To my dear friend
Happy Readi_

With best wishes

Karen

x

My dear infidel
if I have achieved nothing
else in life, at least I will
have served as a bad
example.

HRH
Stella

Living With Infidels:

The Diary of A Saluki – A Hounds Tail

by

Karen Ibbotson

Eloquent Books

Eloquent Books
An imprint of Strategic Book Group
P.O. Box 333
Durham CT 06422
www.StrategicBookGroup.com

ISBN: 978-1-60911-069-7

Printed in the United States of America

Book Design: SP

Dedication

To my beloved family, fellow Infidels and captured Salukis everywhere. With special thanks to all those who have encouraged and supported me. Thank you to my IT Guru for all his hard work, it is appreciated as always.

Table of Contents

Introduction

My family and I are ex pats from the UK, living in Saudi Arabia. Around 2 1/2 years ago, after moving my Weimaraner across the world to Saudi, I realized that he was quite depressed. I decided to look for a companion for him and quite fancied a Saluki having seen them in newspapers here. I started looking on the Internet and doing some research on the breed. I read all kinds of articles and breed descriptions and a Saluki seemed a similar kind of dog to the Weimaraner, aloof, sensitive, and headstrong. Nothing came of my searching for a time, and then after about 6 months I saw a beautiful girl on an ex-pat rescue site and I was hooked. I couldn't stop thinking about her. A lot of cajoling took place to persuade my husband it was a good idea, followed by a few tantrums and a lot of sulking, until he finally caved and let me make the call to the rescue society. Of course I made the call to "enquire", with the full intention of making arrangements to go and collect her! She was living in a foster home in UAE at the time and we had to wait a time while paperwork was completed to bring her over the causeway into KSA.

Finally the day arrived when my husband and I could go and collect her. We drove four hours from Riyadh to Khobar to meet a scraggy little desert bred Saluki bitch that was to transform our lives quite dramatically. I like to think that I am fairly experienced when it comes to dogs, having been owned by 3 Weimaraners and involved in Weimaraner rescue for a time. My parents had dogs when I was growing up and as a teenager I had my own first dog. I did some extensive research on the breed before I made the commitment to take on a Saluki. Nothing, however, quite prepared me for Stella; she came into my life like a whirling dervish. She had a poor beginning to life. She was kept in a pet shop in a crate with her siblings in their own filth. Pet shops here are not like those we know back home. She was underweight, had a broken tail and no fur on her tail, following an injury sustained when another older dog attacked her. She was afraid of everything and so nervous to the point she ripped out her own fur from the stress.

So began a very steep learning curve for me on the road to mending this broken dog. She has to be the most disobedient dog I have come across, and on top of that she suffers from a hormone imbalance. I remember some time last year scoffing bitterly as I read in a book written by a breeder, that a rescue Saluki might be a nice gentle ease into the breed! Hmmm, Stella has been anything but a gentle introduction to the breed, in fact at times she quite frankly is enough to put anyone off Salukis for life! My Weimaraner is quite possibly the most laid back dog alive, he seems to take everything in his stride with stoicism. I am quite sure he rues the day he was ever so depressed that I should seek out a companion for him. I am not sure that Stella was quite the companion he had in mind!

Living with Infidels began as a therapeutic outlet for me to cope with all the things that she throws my way on a daily basis. It is a diary written through the eyes of the majestic Stella, an Arabian princess and captive of us “evil Infidels”. Sadly I must report that all of the events in this book are based actual events, one just couldn’t make this stuff up, nor would you want to!

The face of evil

My slave the kelb

Keeping the kelb in order

Glossary

Kelb – The Arabic word for a common dog, a word, which also means filth. A Saluki is given a different status in Arab culture.
Haram – Forbidden
Ramadan – Muslim religious season of fasting
Infidel – Non-believer
Muttawa – Saudi Religious Police
Kabsah – A dish of meat and rice
Tagine – A type of dish found in North African cuisine, named after the special dish they are cooked in
Imam – An Islamic leadership position, often the leader of a Mosque and community
Arabian Oud – Scented oil
Jihad - An Islamic term for the religious duty of Muslims means "struggle"
Azan – Islamic call to prayers
Abaya – Islamic clothing worn by women to cover the body for modesty
Fatwa - In Islam, a fatwa is a legal decree (it can be a death sentence), which is made by someone who has extensive knowledge of Islamic law.
Hadj - Hadj - the fifth pillar of Islam is a pilgrimage to Mecca during the month of Dhu al-Hijja
Kabbah - The Kabbah is a Giant Stone block in Mecca that all Muslims must pray to at least once in their lifetime.

Stella's Tail

My name is Habibah Nawal, which in Arabic means Beloved Gift. However, the nefarious Infidels that hold me against my will and keep me as their pet have bestowed the hideous appellation of Stella upon me. I believe I am named after their favorite brand of lager, which is an ignominy in itself! When pressed I like to impart the sophisticated version, that I was named after a character in an old movie. This is my story. I couldn't begin writing it in the early days, as it took me a time to learn the Infidel's puerile language. I hope that by documenting the Infidel's atrocities, one day my journal will fall into the right hands and I will be rescued from this life of perpetual perdition at the hands of the diabolical Infidels and their odious kelb. I was meant for greater things! I have a dream that every Saluki is free of the shackles and bonds of the Infidel. I have a dream that no Saluki shall have to endure the perdition of residing with a common kelb. I have a dream that every Saluki is returned to their desert origins. I have a dream and it is a dream of freedom!

Day 346 of Captivity

My many plans for escape have been foiled. The Infidels have taken to spraying me with water for every moment of self-expression. I refuse to recognize the rules; I am a prisoner held captive by Infidels. Their cruelty knows no bounds I am forced to dine on raw chicken and sleep in a quilted crate. I am not allowed to chew on their belongings. This evening's plan was to disgust them beyond belief. I waited until they were dining on their nice smelling food, which looks far more appetizing than mine I hasten to add. Once they were really enjoying their meal I promptly hacked up a large lump of chicken. I then had to ensure the large grey kelb I am forced to share my surroundings with did not swipe the prize. The female Infidel, however, didn't even bat an eyelid and cleaned it up without fuss. Curse these Infidels. Is nothing going to crack them? Will I be forced to live out my days with these wretched folk? My next exploit will not be so easy to deal with; I shall frame the kelb. Mwahahahahahahahaha!

Day 347 Of Captivity

I still remain a captive of the Infidels. Last night the Infidels stayed up very late, which is most unusual for them, they were watching something on the machinery they call a TV. It was midnight when they finally went to sleep. I had had plenty of power naps throughout the evening and it was no problem for me to awake at 2am and urgently request access to the garden. There is a pit in the garden we use for our toilet and the female Infidel had forgotten to clean it yesterday. I thought it rather amusing to pace about looking distressed by this fact, even though there were only 2 soilings in there, until she finally gave in and proceeded to clean the area in the dark. This I found to be excellent entertainment, especially as I could hear the old shrew cursing under her breath, as she stumbled about in the dark trying desperately not to stand in anything grisly. I was then ushered back into the house and my plans of languishing on the Infidel's bed were foiled as she guided me back to my cage. Curse her!

The female Infidel still managed to rise at 5am to exercise the disgusting kelb and I. We are attached to a cycling contraption and we run whilst the female Infidel wallows on the seat of the apparatus spoiling our fun. I find the exercise most satisfactory, what I find very unsatisfactory is the fact that there are many peasant cats on our route and the female Infidel refuses to release us to sort them out. I shout and jump and show my disdain for this act but still she refuses and we are dragged past the smug creatures most unceremoniously. I have concluded that the female Infidel is a buffoon. The kelb insists on marking the route with what he calls his love potion, he too is a buffoon and he smells. Eau de kelb is not a perfume one wishes to inhale I can assure you!

I may spend the day torturing the kelb. I continue to plot from my prison.

Day 347 of captivity - Solitary

I write from the confines of solitary, the Infidels have placed me there for several infractions. I was given a meager meal of raw chicken again this evening while the fat Infidels sat down to a full dinner of wonderful smells. I decided it was only right that they share it with me and stole a chicken carcass that was cooked and seasoned and tasted nice. The male Infidel thwarted my act of theft and retrieved the chicken muttering something about he should have let me choke! These Infidels are treacherous indeed!

I have since performed the wall of death of the lounge; this seems to send the female Infidel into somewhat of a panic as she rushes round the room attempting to secure her many precious things. I always make sure to spring hard on the couch which she seems to find equally upsetting making it all the more pleasurable. This it seems was the straw that broke the camels back this evening and into solitary I was thrust. These Infidels have no sense of adventure and in the evenings all they seem to want to do is lay about watching the machinery called a TV.

The female Infidel has been reading books about my breed and attempting to learn the secrets of the Saluki, never fear as soon as her eye is off the ball I shall eat the books. The secrets of the Saluki are safe with me. Two such attempts have thus far been foiled, but I am not one to give up easily. All the Infidels need to know is that we are complex and to be revered.

I am sad to say that another evening is drawing in and I am still being held against my will. I pass the time by torturing the kelb and the Infidels intermittently. One has to make the tedium pass quickly somehow.

Day 348 of Captivity

I awoke this morning and was dismayed to discover I am still a prisoner of war. The female Infidel has put me in a black mood this morning. As we left the walls of the prison to be exercised on the cycling contraption there was the offspring of a peasant cat opposite the prison running about. There is no place in this world for peasant cats or their filthy offspring. Despite my efforts to free myself I was unable to take it out. I ushered the repugnant kelb into action, but the female Infidel is stronger than I thought and she managed to restrain all 45KG of him!

We continued on our exercise and yet more peasant cats were strolling about like they owned the place. An offspring even dared to dash out in our path and the female Infidel made the cycling contraption come to a screeching halt. She uttered some expletives at the peasant creature, but still she did not free me to assassinate this vermin. This behavior only served to reinforce my opinion that the woman is a buffoon and further blackened my mood. Has she not yet learnt that a Saluki can bear a grudge for days?

On the bright side, today is one of the days that we are visited by another Infidel. This Infidel cleans the prison and I take great delight in toying with her. I must time my torture of her well, because if the female Infidel catches me she will put me in solitary! I play such games as run around the visiting Infidel, which generally releases strange squealing sounds from her and the flapping of arms, excellent fun! I also like to eat her shoes, much to the female Infidel's horror. Thus far I have managed to consume two whole pairs. The female Infidel didn't half go on about this too, something about having to pay for them. I have not paid but the Infidels will and they will pay dearly. Another fun task is to retrieve a feather contraption the visiting Infidel uses to flap around at high objects. I am not as good at this these days. I used to be able to forcibly remove it from her hands, but she is wise to this now and scares me away with whooshing sounds, so I have to bide my time and steal it when it is left unattended. This usually initiates a chase sequence whereby I dart about the house and none of the silly Infidels can catch me. Yes, I am in for a fun day today and perhaps this will serve to lift the black mood that descended on me this morning.

Day 349 Of Captivity - A Glimmer Of Hope

Finally there is a glimmer of hope for my early release from captivity. Whilst exercising this morning we saw some of my fellow countrymen. One of them wished to photograph us. I stood in the background mouthing "HELP ME" but this was to no avail. The female Infidel believes it is because of the novelty of seeing us all on the cycling contraption, but then we all know she is a buffoon! No, I have no doubt in my mind that this document of my plight is winging its way to Amnesty International as I write. Soon a party of rescuers will be dispatched to rescue me from these foul smelling hairless clowns, and this will all be a distant memory. Yes, today I feel the end of captivity draws near. Oh happy day!

Curses! It is a good job Amnesty International are coming soon, the wretched Infidels have found my tunnel I was digging under the prison wall and filled it back in!

Day 350 Of Captivity

My rescuers have not arrived, but I am sure these things take time to organize. As I am in the final days of captivity I thought I would up the ante a little and I spent the evening skulking round the house being as quiet as I could so that the female Infidel would come and investigate. She is just too nosey for her own good that one! A few times I lulled her into a false sense of security by putting on my best innocent face and looking at her questioningly, letting her know that she was wrong to come and look at me so accusingly. The fun part is after she feels guilty, I go and get a shoe out of the shoe rack, which then alerts her suspicions again and makes her all crazy. I sometimes swap this for a tea towel or the dishcloth but I had her running around all night last night. She eventually decided that we would all go to bed as she was fed up of getting up and down all night, she lacks stamina!

I thought I would allow the Infidels to sleep until around 1am when I felt a potter around the garden was in order. A great idea came to me. The female Infidel scrubbed the back yard as the disgusting kelb had made it smell positively nauseating with his so called "love potion". Gag, I cannot imagine what foul creature would be seduced by that vile smell, I really can't! I thought it would be fun to pretend that the smell of disinfectant offended me too much to use our designated area for my "business", so once again I paced the garden looking distressed and then suddenly just went anywhere, which then set the sex crazed kelb into action having to mark over it all with his foul stench. The female Infidel did not look pleased as I left my message right next to the garden seating area they use. She then went out into the garden with more disinfectant to cover it. I love to keep her occupied in the wee hours of the morning. What else would she be doing?

I was once again prevented from languishing on the Infidel's bed after my trip down to the garden. The female Infidel made me return to my cell letting me know there was no way she would trust me to be free in her room whilst she slept. The fat lazy kelb is allowed to wallow on a chaise at night; I mean I am the Princess! He is such a big flabby creep and always looking at them with big dopey eyes and doing their bidding. What a loser!

I am going to power nap now as I may allow them to sleep tonight but then again I may not, it depends on how the mood takes me. I also feel that later today I should draft a letter to some of our world leaders, letting them know what an excellent advisor I would make once they allow me to become a refugee in their country after my rescuers arrive to free me. I think I will start with President Bush, he has nice ears and seems to need all the help he can get! I wonder if all Infidels are buffoons, it seems they are. Also on my short list is that nice chap Mr. Putin, he has an honest face. I really think I should contact whoever is running Britain, the Infidels normally refer to him as "that bloody man!" so I am sure he is a top bloke, as they often refer to me as "that bloody dog!"

Day 352 Of Captivity

I have been too depressed to write for a couple of days, still no sign of a rescue party and I remain a captive of the Infidels. It has been the weekend here; on Wednesday the male Infidel attended a wedding where he met a Prince! I do hope that he put in a good word for me, as I feel a palace would be far more befitting my status as an Arabian princess. I fear that he didn't, no matter how mean I am to these Infidels; they still seem to want to keep me here with them. Perhaps this is their cruel and unusual revenge for my exploits!

The hairy adolescent Infidel went out to babysit and I remained here with the female and the young weedy male Infidel. I like to toy with this male, as he is so lazy he doesn't even use his spine to hold himself up, preferring to loll about the place much to the annoyance of the adult Infidels. This being the case he is far too lazy to reprimand me like the others, so I can jump all over him to my heart's content, providing I choose a time when none of the others see me. I also enjoy overpowering him and taking things from him. The female Infidel keeps telling him that he must be firmer with me or I will take advantage, perhaps she is not quite as stupid I first thought.

The female Infidel is a wily old bird and attempted to weaken my resolve using the skullduggery of cuddles! I only withstood it because it seemed to upset the kelb and make him jealous. She allowed the kelb to come up onto the couch too! He is such a weasel! I decided to show my contempt for them both by lying in a chair alone, throwing them the odd scowl for good measure. It was a late night waiting up for everybody and the female Infidel kept falling asleep on the couch, so to keep her alert I brought the odd shoe from the shoe cupboard and dropped it on her swapping this for a tea towel now and again for variety. Eventually she got a bit annoyed and placed me in solitary.

Once again my attempts at tunneling in the back garden have been sabotaged and they have filled it back in! I find this most annoying! They seem to get very irritated by my excavations.

Last night in an attempt to alleviate my depression, I took a large slab of chocolate cake from the kitchen counter (I had to get it out of the baking tin). Unfortunately, I gave myself away as I took the tea towel used to cover it into the lounge! The female Infidel then placed the cake on top of the refrigerator so that I could no longer reach it. I was a bit gutted as I could have consumed several more pieces. I rounded off the evening by attempting to chew the head off the female Infidel's wooden giraffe. She has had it for some 13 years; high time she replaced it with something new!

This morning the kelb actually managed to astound me with his stupidity! We went out on the cycling contraption as usual and he managed to snap his lead and break free. He stopped so suddenly that his great lumbering force snapped the lead. What did he do with this opportunity? Absolutely NOTHING! He simply trotted alongside the cycling contraption to command and stopped when he was told to! The female Infidel allowed him to complete his exercise in this manner. When he broke free and managed to escape I had a massive hissy fit and tried to escape too. All I managed to achieve was pulling the cycling contraption over and running round in a circle with it, much to the distress of the female Infidel. She had dismounted to check the damage to the lead and see if she could repair it. The kelb truly is an imbecile! I despair!

Day 353 Of Captivity

Today I have had a most displeasing day. The visiting Infidel has been again and she and the female Infidel have caused much disruption to my day! They have moved all of the furniture only to poke around at it with horrid smelling buckets of water, and then they moved it all back again! Buffoons! To illustrate my displeasure, I spent the morning bouncing off all of the furniture and waiting until they had the lounge sufficiently blocked with furniture, so I could crawl underneath it and do naughty things while completely out of reach. I have managed to jump on the coffee table twice today, which really seemed to anger the female Infidel, particularly as she could not get to me. Well let that be a lesson to them, with a bit of luck they have learnt not to disrupt my day in future!

I am now very tired from all my acrobatics and will spend the evening alternating between a deep slumber and fetching shoes from the shoe cupboard. I am still displeased and want the Infidels to feel my ire. The kelb has withered under my gaze; he has spent the day following the female around looking gormlessly at her in between licking the more repulsive parts of his anatomy! Obsequious creature!

PS I have left a message for the gardener to discover in the flowerbed, I do hope he is turning it over by hand again tomorrow. Mwahahahaha

Day 354 Of Captivity

Allah has forsaken me! Several days have passed and still no sign of that elusive rescue party. I remain a prisoner. I have been very weary today after all the upheaval and have spent the day in quiet contemplation, perhaps I need a plan B as the buffoons from Amnesty International clearly do not realize the urgency of my plight! What to do!

I have received a reply from President Bush's Aide. It read as follows:

Dear Stella,

Unfortunately the President does not drive foreign cars; therefore your offer of a Suzuki must be declined. We thank you for your kind offer.

Sincerely,

Office of The Whitehouse

Good grief! I despair, that man seriously needs help! I shall try that nice man Mr. Putin or even Silvio Berlusconi; he likes to surround himself with attractive ladies.

This day has put me in a black mood indeed. Woe-betide the Infidels tomorrow!

Day 356 Of Captivity

Yesterday was a terrible day! The female Infidel was actually my savior! A visiting male Infidel came to the prison yesterday to do some repairs to some wires outside. He then banged on the back door and said he had to come in to do something to a panel in the kitchen. He didn't even wait for the female to put me in the safety of my cell but barged in and I was very frightened. I shouted at him and he kept telling me to go away. The female seemed to be annoyed at this, she took me to the safety of my crate. The visiting male finally left and the female was very angry because he left a mess behind.

She called us to the garden to give us our breakfast as the male had been gone for quite a while and taken all his things with him. I was a little distressed as his scent was in the garden and it made me feel afraid. I finally settled enough to start eating my breakfast when the gate started to open. I ran over and shouted and shouted but the male was back and he just kept coming in and was telling the female to sort us out. The kelb was too busy stuffing his fat face and made sure he finished his breakfast before he joined in the shouting. By now the female Infidel had become quite irate and she shouted at the male to get out! He went outside and the female went out too and shouted at him a lot! He waited outside while the female took me to the safety of my crate, only then did she allow the male Infidel to enter, by now his demeanor had changed somewhat and he sounded very whiney and apologetic.

The male was here a while doing repairs but this time he did not barge in he knocked and asked first and he didn't dare tell the female to sort us out. He eventually left and never returned but his visit put me in a dither all day and every little thing sent me running for the safety of my crate. I did not feel happy at all in the garden for the rest of the day and did not eat anything yesterday, because I was too worked up. I did find some copper wiring which I attempted to eat but the female Infidel caught me and retrieved it, she then began to curse the visiting male once more. He really has caused trouble here today!

The female went to bed early as we have an early start. I was still very shaken up and she allowed me to lie with her on their bed wrapped in their downy. I liked this it felt safe and secure and I calmed down. Once I felt happy again I went to my crate to sleep, because I was too hot.

After the stress of yesterday I am feeling quite hyper today so to run off some of my energy I have been doing laps of the prison, up and down the stairs and round and round the rooms. The female does not seem as disturbed by this behavior today so perhaps I will take advantage. I will see how far she will allow me to go.

Day 358 Of Captivity

Saudi religious police ban pet cats and dogs - Yahoo! News UK

I don't believe it! The Muttawa have passed a law that there will be no pet dogs or cats in Riyadh. Peasant cats I can understand, as they are disgusting and have no place on Allah's clean Earth. Dogs! Surely they mean kelb's and not the chosen ones! And what is this word pet? Surely they mean fellow inmates, captives of the cruel Infidel society.

The Infidel's cruelty knows no bounds they have only fed me twice today. When I helped myself to a wad of lasagna sheets someone had casually discarded in the kitchen, I was brutally wrestled to the ground and my food was confiscated, I was then subjected to solitary! All the while the vacant kelb sat grinning inanely and drooling outside my cell. He really is disgusting! Gag!

Perhaps this new law is an opportunity for escape and to be finally reunited with my Bedouin brothers and sisters. Apparently, the "pets" in question are to be confiscated if caught; now all I have to do is convince the female buffoon to exercise me in the middle of town.

Day 360 Of Captivity

When will these fatuous Infidels learn that I wish to dine on Lamb Kabsah and dates and not their disgusting unseasoned raw chicken or lambs offal that they keep serving up? I am not meant for this! Why do they think that I want to dine al fresco? I should be fanned and hand served and certainly should not have to share my eating space with a fat drooling kelb. I only consume the chicken to annoy him, as he is constantly poised ready to scoff anything that I do not eat. To show my disdain for their measly offerings I hacked up a large chicken leg on their carpet this evening and to my absolute horror the drooling minion ate it! Are there no levels that he will not stoop to? He eats things that would make a Billy goat puke!

Perhaps this show of defiance will let them know I am not happy with their so-called food. I do like to do this now and again to drive the message home that I do not care for raw chicken and would have much preferred to consume the chicken tagine that the fat Infidels quaffed.

I was engaging in some good humored banter with one of the gardeners through the prison windows this morning when the male Infidel threatened through gritted teeth to slap the fur out of me if I uttered another sound! He apparently was engaged in some feeble minded activity on the computer thing that I am not allowed to touch. I may wee on it tomorrow, to let him know I am not impressed. After dragging a few papers out of the office and getting sprayed with water, I went into my cell and sulked all afternoon, not that anyone noticed.

Day 362 Of Captivity

I was gaily singing along to the Imam calling to prayers at 4am this morning in my best singing voice, but the Infidels did not appear to appreciate my musical talent. They awoke in the foulest of tempers! The black mood continued when the female Infidel took us for a run on the cycling contraption this morning. The filthy kelb decided to evacuate his bowels on route and while the female was cleaning up the foul mess, I started leaping about excitedly as I had seen a peasant cat and wished for her to release me to assassinate it. With all my activity I almost made her fall in the kelb's leavings, which did not seem to make her very happy. She muttered some unrepeatable words for the rest of the exercise and seemed to be in a very bad mood when we returned to the prison!

I am not very pleased this morning either, because the female Infidel has stripped all my bedding and is putting it in the machine that she thinks makes it smell nice! I can see that I will have to do something about that, as I prefer my bedding to have a more Saluki aroma to it. A bit of Arabian Oud sprayed in my cell would go down a treat but no; I have to have Infidel smells of jasmine and magnolia from their machine instead.

I have spent the morning chewing on a rug on the landing as no one is paying me any attention. I even left a bit of the wool on the corner of my mouth so that they would know. Yes that got their attention. I am now in solitary just for a change. Bugger!

Day 365 of Captivity

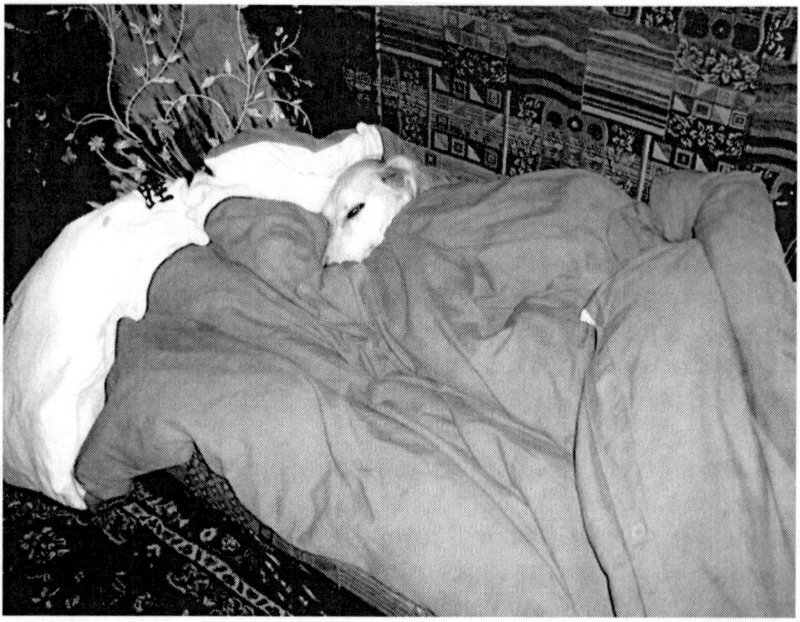

It is very tiring being *this* evil. The Infidels have taken a week of holiday and I am taking the opportunity to power nap as much as possible in order that I may continue to annoy them on a greater level once the household returns to normal. I have had some serious naps!

Day 372 Of Captivity

Groan! I am still a captive! We had an eventful week last week. A video was made of us exercising but after last time I don't hold out much hope of anything coming of it! Amnesty International is clearly populated with Infidels and they are all in it together. I still await their arrival with baited breath!

The kelb managed to wangle a trip to the centre of town but you have all guessed it, he returned with the Infidels. He was none too pleased as he had had a needle stuck in his posterior and was no fun all day, as he just wanted to sleep. I protested quite vigorously at not being taken along on this trip, although I am pleased that I did not have a needle stuck anywhere in me! These Infidels are degenerates!

Whilst the visiting Infidel was here at the weekend, she opened the front door not long after the Infidels had left the house. The kelb always snivels when they leave and he decided to jump over the visiting Infidel and go after them. He is such a moron though he made it into the light of day and to freedom and then came back in the house again! I tell you if you get close enough to his head you can hear the air whistling through, he is like a living conch!

So, another day in this dull Infidel world for me!

Day 373 Of Captivity

May the fleas of a thousand camels infest their armpits, a Jihad on them all and their sweaty kelb! Following our exercise on the cycling contraption this morning the female Infidel decided to return to bed because she felt unwell (yawn). I just think she is a lazy witch. The big fat creepy kelb was languishing on the bed next to her and when I attempted to torment him by chewing his ears, I was placed in my cell! I made sure that they didn't get very much sleep by singing my version of the Azan from my solitary confinement. Every time the female Infidel told me to shut up, I sang louder and shriller grating on her eardrums, until she eventually released me and gave up on the idea of sleep.

I was not satisfied with my exercise today even though it was as much as we usually get, that and being caged has irritated me. To show my displeasure I have spent the day careering around the house at top speed bouncing off various pieces of furniture and leaving skid marks in all of the carpets, that is until the female Infidel became so incensed she threatened to rip my ears off and placed me in solitary to apparently calm down and settle. It was a good opportunity to plot my next move.

Once I was released from solitary for a second time today I sulked for a time on the landing to give the impression their feeble punishment had been a success. Once they were satisfied that I had learnt my lesson I meandered into the lounge and chewed the camel saddle for a while. I was sprayed in the head with water for this infraction so I moved on to chew the sofa cushion, until I gave myself away by being a little over zealous and making a noise! I received a telling off from the irksome female Infidel. I am now posting a vigil at the prison window hoping that someone will spot my despondent face and save me from this wretched existence. I keep shouting to passers by, but they just accelerate up the street looking startled! Cretins! It is probably the kelb's fault, because he has joined in a few times and he has a big mouth and just sounds clinically insane! I have told him this but am simply met by a blank stare. I wonder if his ears are broken? Hmm maybe I should chew them a little less.

Day 376 Of Captivity

Not only do these Infidels feed me the most disgusting gruel of raw chicken, but now they have cut my portions down, because the female Infidel thinks that my posterior is becoming bulky. Smacks somewhat of the pot calling the kettle don't you think? After my meager rations this morning I was still feeling famished, so I dined on her knee brace. Maybe she will realize that I am starving here!

Last night when the Infidels were carrying out their various evening ablutions before retiring I managed to secure the prime spot on the Infidel's bed. The male was none too happy about this and when he attempted to remove me to my cell I hung like a sack of potatoes, during the ensuing wrestling I managed to place my foot in his mouth, more than once, which I had made sure was coated in the kelb's foul urine while I was in the garden before being forced to retire for the night.

I note from the newspapers with dismay Saudi Arabia has not fielded a ladies' team for the Olympics, I am ready to pick up the baton. I thought they would have, as my sisters all look quite muscular underneath their abayas and appear to give the men a good hiding at the slightest provocation. Mind you if I was dressed from head to foot in black in these temperatures, my mood would be somewhat crabby too! However, the color is very slimming. I could probably outrun any number of the fat Infidels taking part in these events with very little effort. Even the Kelb would be good, if there were an event for sniffing posteriors, licking one's foul anatomy or standing still looking vapid, he would win gold every time!

Anyway I must go and continue my preparations for Ramadan, which include singing the Azan 24 hours a day. The infidels will just love it!

Day 377 of Captivity

There is no end to the lengths these Infidels will go to, to torture me! Not only are they continuously putting their foul breathed faces near my head and kissing me (Gag! The indignity!), patting me and patronizing me with comments like "Aren't you a pretty girl?" Of course I am beautiful! I am a princess! They insist on grooming my coat as well to make me look like I belong in this Infidel society, as their prisoner. The female Infidel spent some time this afternoon smoothing down my unruly coat and I now have to spend my energy trying to cultivate the unkempt look again! Perhaps there will be something nasty in the garden I can roll in to undo her labor and return myself once more to the free spirit that I truly am. Next time she leaves the drawer of dog equipment open, I am going to eat the grooming tools!

Day 380 of Captivity

I have discovered that the neighbors across the street from the prison speak Arabic! A couple of days ago I went into the bedroom upstairs so that I would have a better view of their abode. Every time one of them moved about in their house I screamed at the top of my voice "help me, HELP ME!" I felt sure that they would hear me and see my predicament. However, the fat sweaty kelb came in when I was screaming and shouted over the top of my voice with his bellowing voice, singing like a canary and alerting the buffoon Infidels to my escape attempt. So once again all the neighbors could hear was the insane ranting of the local lunatic kelb! He needs to be on medication. The curtains were closed and I could make no further pleas for help from my potential saviors.

Needless to say I am still a captive of the filthy Infidels. I have not given up on the neighbors; I just need to find a way to silence the kelb! He is such a big fat snitch!

Day 384 of Captivity

This week the Infidels announced that they were holding a dinner party, I awaited my invitation with glee knowing that they could not fail to invite such an important and prestigious guest as myself, a pure bred Arabian princess, only to discover it was for buffoons only with the exception of my fellow Arab neighbors.

Last night the Infidels hosted the dinner party. The neighbors from across the street were on the guest list. However, the Infidels have got wise to my plans of speaking to them, so they kept me away from them by placing me in solitary for the evening and my chances of engaging in witty repartee and human rights abuses within the prison were dashed. This solitary confinement may also have something to do with the fact that over the duration of the day they were very busy and somewhat fraught and in order to return their focus on ME, where it clearly belongs, I ate a dish cloth, shredded a sponge, stole and chewed 3 napkin rings and the napkins therein. I also chased the visiting Infidel around the house a couple of times. The fat kelb drove me insane pacing incessantly around the house looking vacuous.

The Infidels and their guests sat down and quaffed a huge feast of tagines and rice, sweets and soup and I was given a grimy bone to chew on in the afternoon and 2 dates from one of the guests, a fellow Arab, who took pity on my emaciated form and could clearly see I was starving and ill treated having to contend with living with these irksome Infidels. My shrill cries for help were ignored all evening, as was my rendition of various Bedouin folk songs in my efforts to entertain and be part of this event.

I have taken my revenge today by defecating on the doorstep just outside the back door, much to the irritation of the male Infidel. The kelb has shunned me all day despite my attempts to engage him in a spot of Arabic wrestling. I remain a prisoner of buffoons.

Day 387 of Captivity

...Look what those wretched degenerate Infidels have done to me now!

I then had to endure thirty minutes of being brushed and I smell of oatmeal and tea tree, GAK! Oh someone is going to pay for this most disgraceful violation against my person.

The only bonus was that their fat, smelly kelb had to have a bath as well and now he is a little more tolerable to be around, it took some shampoo to get rid of his smell I can tell you! Being the big creep he is, he jumped in and out of the bath for the female Infidel. It is a good job; it would take half an hour of tears and a carton of "Chunky Monkey" to recover from lifting his corpulent carcass into the bath! I made sure to grab the doorframe on the way into the bathroom and spread all four paws on the sides of the bath to ensure bathing me was a most difficult task. I also made sure to shake all the water off onto the female Infidel before she managed to get a towel.

How *very* dare she! I am now lay under the dining table plotting my revenge. I keep throwing her the odd withering stare. May her abaya be infested with the stench of a thousand haddocks!

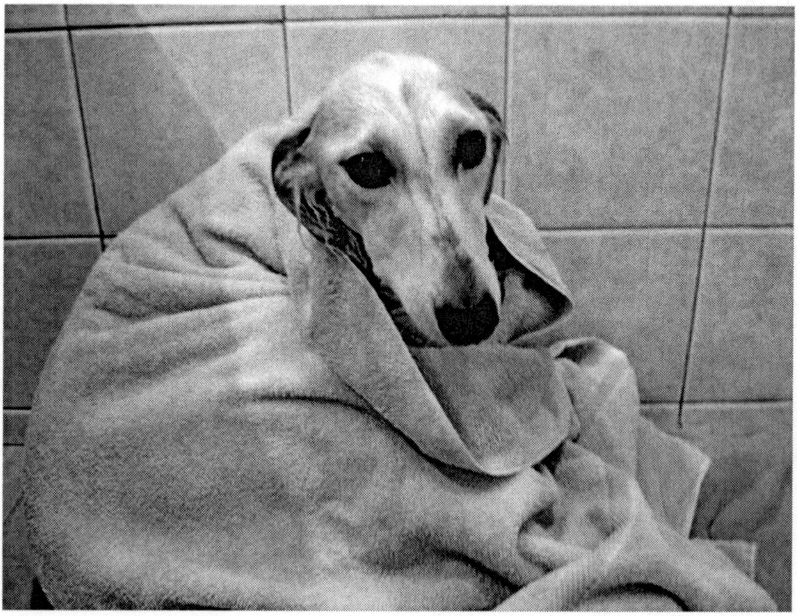

Day 388 of Captivity

Revenge is a dish best served cold. I woke the Infidels at 2.30 this morning to demand my breakfast, as I must be fed before sun up. Being the buffoons they are, they simply threw me out into the garden and sent me in the direction of the toilet area! When I was put back in my cell I thought a bit of singing was in order, but thought it prudent to fall silent when the male Infidel threatened to bury me in the desert. He is prone to bouts of rage, particularly if woken in the wee hours of the morning!

We have had our daily exercise and a couple of hours later the Infidels fed me! I refused to indulge them. It is Ramadan! Now I shall have to wait until sun down to be sated, cretins! Needless to say the fat Infidel kelb quaffed his meal this morning.

I am currently languishing on the Infidel's bed, but no doubt they will find some asinine excuse to put me in my cell. The usual crimes are running around the room at top speed, wrestling with the kelb when he is sleeping, jumping on their heads when they are trying to sleep and other such trivial excuses. Why don't they just have me stuffed and be done with it?

Day 390 of Captivity

Yesterday not only did the big clumsy oaf Infidel kelb almost have my eye out with his fat feet during a spot of wrestling I initiated but the female Infidel, not satisfied with this attack, also tried to execute me yesterday! She administered some medication to allegedly worm me; princesses do not have worms! I spent the day out in the disgusting toilet area or weeping under the dining table.

I managed to muster the strength to chew up a permanent marker in the hairy adolescent Infidel's room, getting green ink all over his rug and unfortunately all over my legs. A pitiful effort I know but I was frail and debilitated by the female Infidel's toxins.

I am feeling much brighter this morning. I ensured that the female Infidel was unable to return to bed after our exercise this morning, by running around the house at top speed and fetching the tea towel and dishcloth in and out of the kitchen. Once I ensured she was completely awake, I decided to retire to my bed and sleep. I will probably sleep for much of the day now. The female Infidel does not look too amused, as I believe she was very tired this morning. What a shame! Perhaps she will have second thoughts before attempting to dispatch me in future!

Day 393 of Captivity

The buffoon female Infidel took some photos of me wearing a silly pink coat that I believe is to be my winter attire this year, or at least she thinks so anyway!

I refused to pander to her silliness and would not look into the camera.

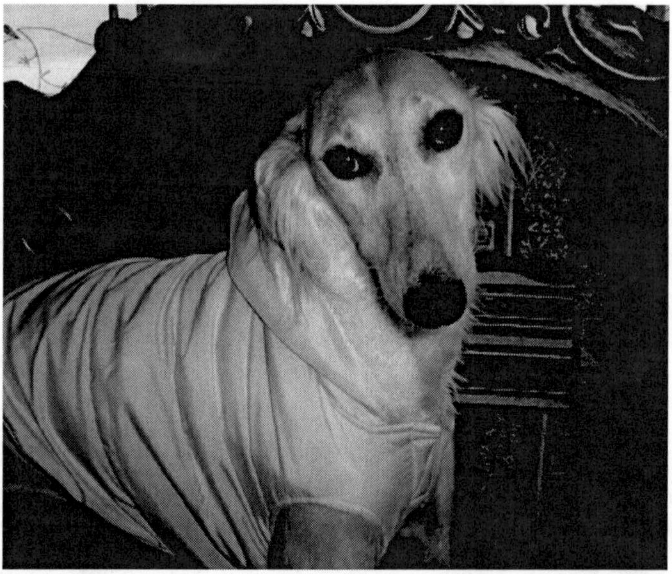

Of course being a fabulous princess it was a little difficult to resist.
(Look at my tortured face).

I am acutely aware that I look a complete imbecile in this hideous Infidel contraption! I am not amused!

I am just trying to work out if there is any way that I can consume this coat to spare myself the humility of having to wear it in public.

You have witnessed the torture they put me through, if anyone out there wishes to emancipate me, please do! Infidels need not apply!

Day 404 of Captivity

Ramadan Kareem! I have been quiet of late as it is the festival of Ramadan. I have spent much of my time sleeping during the day, waking late afternoon to attain a sugar rush from dates, I haven't managed to get my hands on any coffee, the Infidels keep it hidden and make comments along the lines of me being wired enough!

I have managed to consume yet another of the visiting Infidel's pairs of shoes, which made the female Infidel extremely angry. She can be a drama queen that one! I got hold of their music machine remote today and attempted to annihilate it, there is only so much Abba a girl can stand!

The Infidels went out this evening and I was left behind with the teenage hairy hormonal Infidel and the weedy stringy little Infidel, who tastes unclean. I amused myself springing into the weedy ones room and relieving him of his possessions and myself on his carpet. This was a great source of entertainment until the hairy one flew into a hormonal outburst and I was thrust once more into solitude. He really needs to chill out a bit and get a sense of humor! Still I doubt if I would have a sense of humor if I resembled a tactically shaved chimp!

Day 415 of Captivity

The male Infidel has taken the hairy teen and the nerdy boy Infidels away on holiday for 18 days. The female Infidel has remained at home with the sweaty kelb and myself, apparently many of her friends would be willing to take the kelb but they are all too lily-livered to cope with me! How feeble they must be!

I have been keeping the female on her toes and dug a nice big crater in the back yard, which she consequently filled back in. I have pretended to be restless at the departure of the male Infidels and used it as an excuse to chew on a few things. Quite frankly I wish they had all gone away, I could then live the life I was born for and enjoy a bit of freedom, instead of having to endure the tedium of these wretched proles. I shall enjoy bringing the female Infidel to her knees over the next week or so; normally she has reinforcements, let's see how she copes with me on her own.

Day 418 of Captivity

The visiting Infidel is here again today. She has vexed me considerably this morning. I was enjoying a morning slumber, when the visiting Infidel decided to Hoover the couch on which I was taking my nap and rudely awakened me! Such insolence! This injustice prompted me to consume yet another of her shoes, to let her know that I was scandalized by her impudence! Needless to say the female Infidel was outraged by my act of revenge and I, the injured party, was sent to solitary with a severe reprimand. Hardly just!

I let the female Infidel know that I am brooding by letting out very long and dramatic sighs. She will suffer for this injustice later. I will wait until she is tired and then antagonize her. I have many weapons in my arsenal that I can bombard her with.

Day 422 of Captivity

I have had such fun for the last few days, all at the female Infidel's expense of course. She and her friend have started making Christmas decorations! Every Infidel knows full well that Christmas is haram! She spent ages sticking little trees onto a skirt that is to go round her tree, and I managed to get hold of it the other day and bite a few off. She was not at all amused, as it had taken the best part of an afternoon to put them there. She bellowed at me when she caught me, she really must learn not to leave things lying about even if it for just a few seconds, I am a fast worker.

Last night was not so much fun, I seem to be experiencing another hormone surge and the kelb was like a dog possessed. He seemed to be of the opinion that I was his prison bitch yesterday; the mere thought sends a shiver down my spine and makes me feel sick to the stomach. Not even if he were the last kelb alive would I sully myself so! Luckily the female Infidel removed him and made him lie down away from me, it didn't stop his attempts on my person, and it was as if he were bewitched. I can understand his attraction to me, I am rather alluring, but he is a minion. GAK!

The dust seems to have settled this morning and he has only had a quick sniff as the female told him at once to leave me. I just know that if it continues I will have to be taken to see the Vet and be impaled again with a needle to stop the hormones. What a wretched existence. A fatwa on the lustful kelb! Loathsome creature.

Day 427 of Captivity

The female Infidel seemed to become slightly enraged this morning when I ran away with the shower curtain, complete with pole, during her shower. I managed to hit her on the head with the pole as I made my escape, perhaps it will knock some sense into her! I attempted to run through the door with it, but I miscalculated the gap in the door and was bounced back into the bathroom to be faced with a grisly vision. She was covered in soap and shampoo and screeching at me, she looked like an abomination, the sight was quite abhorrent and I soon began to regret this maneuver. She really ought to have grasped the fact that I become very bored when left alone for even a few moments! This week I have managed to gnaw on her mobile phone, shred a box of tissues and steal the shower curtain all during shower time, does anyone else see a theme here? Yes the female Infidel truly is a dullard!

Oh well a little amusement to start off another dull day in the tedious world of the proles. I still remain a captive of the Infidels after all these long months and I despair of there ever being a rescue party. One has to amuse oneself somehow during these dark days!

Day 442 of Captivity

Oh what glee! The male Infidel and his hairy offspring have returned from their holiday bringing with them suitcases full of new and interesting items for me to chew. I have my eye on a set of wooden elephants; the chewing opportunity is just too good to pass up. Thus far I have not been able to get near them without the female Infidel flailing her arms about and shrieking at me like a demented banshee that I *will* be taken to the desert! Does she not realize this is what I have been waiting for all these long dark months? It seems all that it would take is to chew those elephants. I am, however concerned that my trip to the desert is also mentioned in the same sentence as shovels and deep cavernous holes.

Yawn! The Infidels are very pleased with themselves, they spent the weekend installing wooden blinds at the windows and ever since I have not been permitted to even get so much as my nose near the windows without the onset of bouts of rage and mass hysteria! I am very peeved! They don't seem to comprehend that they require my skills as a sentry to keep away any peasant cats and other subordinate creatures that pass by the windows without permission. There is also the issue of those grubby men that turn up three times a week and steal our garbage!

To top it all off a new lounge suite was delivered this morning and it appears that all gymnastic activities and walls of death have been suspended indefinitely. My Infidel hell just became the most tedious place on earth. My only source of entertainment has been that the moronic kelb has not been able to decide whether he is allowed to lie on the new furniture or not and the Infidels don't seem to be letting on either. I am currently scoffing at him from the sofa, as he lies drooling on the floor. Most amusing!

Day 451 of Captivity

This morning after our exercise on the cycling contraption the female Infidel let me out into the garden. She was not as vigilant as she usually is and I managed to consume some umbrella grass. Once I was discovered I was ushered back into the house and the female Infidel had a face like thunder. We went back to bed for a while as we had got up very early to exercise, I managed to secure a spot on the bed this morning and was enjoying languishing, scoffing at the kelb on his bed.

I waited until the female Infidel had drifted off and then I jumped off the bed and began to pace the bedroom looking for a suitable bit of carpet to deposit the regurgitated umbrella grass. I must have been a bit over zealous, as the noise I was making alerted the female Infidel. There is nothing quite like the power of the sound of a retching dog to get an Infidel up and moving, they seem to develop super speed! I must say she has to be applauded for the speed in which she thrust me into the en suite throwing bath mats left, right and centre as she went. I had no other choice but to deposit the vomit onto the tiled floor of the bathroom. Not quite the victorious Technicolor yawn I envisaged for her carpets and the ensuing hysteria that it would have incited.

I felt slightly triumphant as I watched the female wretched at having to clean up the slimy mess from the tiles, whilst swearing under her breath, flapping her arms at the disgusting kelb who has been known to dine on my vomit on more than one occasion! That beast would eat things that would make a Billy goat gag!

Needless to say my languishing was over and it was back to the cell for me. Still I took solace in the fact I had clearly upset the female Infidel at an early hour of the day; a minor victory but I will take it.

I have been annoying her this morning by standing at the window on the precious new furniture, and every time she gets off her seat to remove me I jump down, only to jump back up when she returns to her seat at the computer book thing she spends her time "working" on. She took this for a time and then sent me to my crate, as she is clearly too lazy to keep getting up and down!

The tedium continues!

Day 452 of Captivity

I knew that the Infidels were complete and utter simpletons, but I am now convinced that they don't have an ounce of sense! The world has been coming to an end and they have sat around drinking tea as if nothing were happening. There have been flashes of light in the sky, loud bangs and rumblings and the sky has been collapsing since yesterday, water has been gushing from the heavens. I am doomed to die as an Infidel captive! Is there no end to the humiliation I must endure! I have been hiding in my crate and the kelb has taken refuge under the dining table. Death amongst these godless rogues must surely mean that I will not get into heaven, instead I will end my days surrounded by their pling pling gods and joss sticks.

Day 463 of Captivity

I was just alerting the female Infidel to the fact that she had shut me out of the bedroom this morning, when she thrust the door open and ambushed me. I was unceremoniously plunged into the bath and scrubbed clean, in tea tree and oat shampoo! Since when has a Royal Saluki aspired to smell of tea tree? Curses!

The torture then continued as she cleaned my ears. I was rather vexed by this dastardly act. To pay her back for this treachery I did the wall of death of the lounge, bouncing hard on the new precious furniture. This sent the female Infidel into an apoplectic fury, which resulted in me once again being thrust into solitary in a most undignified fashion. In the hopes of giving her a heart attack or making her actually implode I then vomited on the carpet the instant I was released. I have spent the afternoon on the sofa with a look of smug glee on my face.

The only saving grace to this entire sorry episode was that the sweaty kelb was also tortured. He smells less like a decomposing badger, and one can be in his presence without feeling the urge to gag violently. Although, he still has the breath from Satan's buttocks! The horror...The horror!

Day 485 of Captivity

Scoff! The Infidels have truly surpassed themselves this time, I really didn't believe they could be any more fatuous, but once again they have proved me wrong. They have erected a 7ft tree inside the house, yes you heard me right, and it is actually INSIDE the house! It appears to be in celebration of that heathen festival Christmas! I am rather disappointed that the kelb has not tried to urinate on it even once; which is very out of character for him. That buffoon will urinate on just about anything, including on occasion ME!

I have made many valiant attempts to sabotage this atrocity that now adorns our living room with its vulgar shiny embellishments and hideous flashing lights. I have driven the female Infidel to the brink of insanity with my efforts; a favorite is to eat the tinsel she really gets upset by this. I have produced some very festive excreta in the last few weeks, complete with shiny bits of tinsel. Hang that on your tree Infidels!

The female Infidel is being very jolly and listening to tiresome tunes by worn out old has-beens, such as Cliff Richards. If I hear Mistletoe and Wine one more time, I swear I will chew off my own ears! Oh, the monstrous torment these Infidels put me through is inhumane!

Of course it is Hadj, but instead of going on a pilgrimage to the Holy Land, I am to be left here surrounded by Christmas trees and bloody Father Christmas! I must have been truly evil in a former life to deserve the infinite perdition that is to be my daily life. I am going to wait until no one is looking and shred the Christmas presents, they will not enjoy this heretical affair. How very dare they! Allah be praised and deliver me from these Infidels. I pray that the New Year brings opportunities for my emancipation.

Day 492 of Captivity

As I lay pouting on the couch saddened at not being able to attend Hadj AGAIN, I am spurred on by the thought that at least I annoy the Infidels. The female Infidel in a pathetic attempt to cheer me up left a black shoebox lying in the dining room. I think the thought was if I closed my eyes and ran round it, I would imagine the thrill of mixing with millions of true believers making our way around the Kabbah, instead I ate the shoes and chewed the box. How lame is she?

She went out this morning to meet with fellow Infidels and consume coffee and quaff cakes! She seems to be attempting to match her own body weight when consuming the cakes. I myself have found a new game to play with the kelb; it is called "Torture the Kelb with food". I wait for the imbecile to devour his chicken, all the while skulking round the garden pretending to sniff the flowers. Once he has finished I very, very slowly savor my chicken, enjoying every mouthful, whilst the drooling buffoon looks on. I particularly enjoy it when he attempts to help me with my meal and consequently he is unceremoniously stuffed in the kitchen to drool through the screen door. It is hilarious! One thing though, I almost died slipping in a river of his foul drool, what an embarrassing way to go! The sheer horror of being found in such a way by fellow peers!

I have actually managed to languish on the Infidel's bed these past few nights. I have to be careful to remain still until I hear the dulcet tones of the male Infidel sucking in the room with his thunderous snores. The sound would put a rhino to shame! The nasal symphony is quite ghastly! In fact it vexed me so much last night, I was compelled to go into my crate of my own volition. As soon as the female heard me hit the back of the crate she leapt from her bed and locked me in, muttering something about my having been flapping about like a salmon! Still, I would rather be a salmon than a trout old bean!

Day 498 of Captivity

This year I have mostly been eating:

1 camel saddle
7 pairs of shoes
1 mobile phone
2 pairs of spectacles
3 of the legs from a wooden elephant
2 TV remotes
2 kitchen chairs
A trashy novel
Pot pourri
A brightly colored pen (managed to get the ink on the carpet with that one)
An Umbrella plant
Several yards of tinsel
A blanket
All of the sweaty kelb's toys (he should not be so pitiful and run round with cuddly toys)
Cushion covers
Tassels from cushions
The curtains on the landing
The tiebacks on the landing
The rug on the landing (bit of a clue here, supervise me on the landing!)
The face off a sock monkey (I was disturbed mid chew and did not manage to fully consume this item)
1 DVD
Several TV guides
Various invertebrates found in the garden
Various dishcloths and sponges (I particularly like the green scrubby variety of sponge if anyone is thinking of a Christmas gift!)

Much counter surfing activity has taken place this year and I have managed to surreptitiously liberate several doughnuts from being scoffed by the Infidels (I am only thinking of their girth)

And a Weim mar rah ah ah ner (hmm it works to the tune of the 12 days of Christmas)

Yes, all in all it has been a good year for consumables. May 2009 bring more of the same.

Day 505 of Captivity

Well I'll be damned; this heathen festival of Christmas has not been so bad after all, in that it has provided many opportunities for food thievery and skullduggery. The Female Infidel does seem to have placed me under a close supervision order these past few days, which I find rather exasperating! I was just unwrapping my second Quality Street chocolate this afternoon, which I had looted while she was otherwise engaged; but unfortunately she returned to the room and caught me in the act. I made her chase me round the furniture to retrieve it, leaving her a gasping heap on the couch as I sprang gracefully round the coffee table. She is about as agile as a wounded rhino!

This festival seems to be a time for leaving plates piled high with copious amounts of wonderful smelling food just lying about the place to be pilfered. The boring fat kelb never takes anything, even when it is right there asking to be liberated. He almost caved at lunchtime when it came to the cheese board, flapping his tongue about in the distance! How vapid of him, he is a large dog and could easily overpower any of the Infidels and just take it, but he is too busy being a big fat creep. He sits and gives them a paw for goodness sake. The Infidels seem to absolutely lap this up and give him the odd tidbit here and there. I would never descend to such degradation!

I have managed to purloin the odd mince pie and chocolate here and there. Christmas morning was marvelous, apart from an appalling beginning to the day whereby the female served me up with a plate of turkey giblets! She was so pleased with this abysmal offering it was really quite tragic. Of course the kelb devoured the lot with glee. He really is an abomination!

The day did pick up, however, when I "assisted" the hairy Infidel and his weedy sibling in opening their gifts by dashing past them and ripping great lumps of paper off for them, which I then did a lap of victory of the coffee table with. I had a blast. It did seem to irk the adolescents, so somewhat of a bonus!

The drawback to the day was that I was put into solitary once it was time to serve up the mouth-watering meal that they all quaffed. The miserable Infidels got irritated because I was circling the dining table like a shark. It smelled so good, much better than the abhorrent gruel that was bestowed upon me this morning. They must have been consumed with guilt for their cruelty, because after they had eaten I was given a lovely big bowl of cooked turkey, which I have to say I thoroughly enjoyed. Now what I would like to know is, why can't they feed me like that everyday!

Day 515 of Captivity

I have not been very well over the Christmas period; it is entirely the Infidel's fault for leaving such niceties lying about just asking to be consumed. As a result the evil Infidels decided to starve the kelb and I for 24 hours. To exact my revenge for their callousness, I woke them in the early hours of the morning gagging, having nothing to sustain me, but my hatred of the Infidels. It was my 2nd birthday that morning as well!

I was fed a meager meal of gruel of raw chicken after suffering at the hands of the diabolical Infidels, hardly recompense! I stored their monstrous behavior to use against them later. The opportunity arose to retaliate this evening and I regurgitated my ghastly meal of chicken onto their much-prized Indian carpet. The fun then began as the female Infidel attempted to wrestle the big fat kelb to the ground before he banqueted on my leavings. I decided to fight the kelb just to add even more amusement to the situation. The female was not amused and exploded into a fit of apoplexy. The kelb astutely made his exit and let the female clean up what was left. I was sent to the solitary confinement of my crate.

Not satisfied with my counterattack on the Infidels, I waited until they were engrossed in the television and took my opportunity for some further skullduggery. While I was left in solitary the Infidels had dined on some nice smelling homemade herby chicken nuggets. I thought the oil they were cooked in smelt rather good so managed a good 5 minutes drinking it. The female Infidel was absolutely horrified when she walked in on me! It appears that the last laugh is on me though, I am now confined to the couch with the most frightful bellyache and they don't even care that I am crying! The male Infidel even said that it was my own fault! Perhaps I will turn the tables and wake them at dawn with some serious retching, see which of us is laughing then!

Day 519 of Captivity

The hairy adolescent Infidel tried to kill me this evening! I was just about to tuck into the weedy one's pudding, when he shrieked at the top of his voice and almost gave me a heart attack! I was so shocked I almost dropped the mouthful of toffee pie I had sequestered! I was forced to bolt my second mouthful as he began to wave his arms around in an alarming manner. It is all rather disconcerting when one is trying to eat!

The male Infidel took pity on me and gave me some of his ice cream. This does not mean that I like him and I will continue to eviscerate his underwear wherever and whenever I find it.

I managed to add to the kelb's already disturbed state of mind by draping myself around his neck this evening and biting a lump from the corner of his eye. The big Jesse just lay there and allowed me to maul him. I told him to man up! He remains hopeful that his brawny, untalented advances will one day seduce me. Quite frankly I would rather be flayed alive and rolled in Marmite! GAK! He is truly repellent!

Day 526 of Captivity

Consumables of 2009:
1 Satellite TV control
1 Coaster
1 watchstrap

I like to keep my diet mixed and varied.

I almost managed to maim the male Infidel this evening. He was throwing himself about on this new electric running machine they have bought. I was stood at the foot of the belt contemplating what would happen if I stepped on the end during his run, when the female caught me and flapped her arms about to make me move. They are always flapping about; it is most annoying. I assume that my stepping on the end of the belt mid run would have had dire consequences for the male Infidel, perhaps I will store this one for another day, when the pesky female is not there to interrupt me.

Day 533 of Captivity

This week I have mostly been eating spectacles:
1 pair of sunglasses belonging to a visiting Infidel (sequestering visiting Infidel's possessions always has the maximum impact and causes the most fuss!)
1 Pair of spectacles belonging to the male Infidel
1 pair of spectacles belonging to the weedy adolescent Infidel

I have relished in infuriating the female Infidel this week. I am experiencing a "pseudo season" at the moment, which is a great excuse to behave restlessly and partake in much skullduggery. Pacing relentlessly about the prison, looking shifty usually results in a bout of rage from either the female who has spent much of the day supervising my pacing (she doesn't appear to trust me out of her line of sight!) or the male who is "weary from a days work". Unfortunately this then results in solitary confinement for me. I do glean some satisfaction from bringing them to the brink of rage at times. I can then sit in my cell and plot my next assault.

I have managed to sequester several pairs of spectacles this week, however, I have not managed to eviscerate them thanks to the constant shadow of bore that follows me around all day in the form of the female Infidel. Quite a frightening form she is too! Her grating voice and tedious demeanor, she never lets me have any fun! Every little expression of freedom is quashed. Only this afternoon I was dragging my bedding from my crate, as I was most put out that it had been washed. I was going to drag it through the garden and get it nice and pungent again, but oh no the shadow of bore protested as usual! YAAAAAAAAAAAWN!

I have taken to singing along to various theme tunes on the television, much to the displeasure of the Infidels. I can reach some really high notes as well, but as usual being completely dreary the Infidels hate it. They say my voice pierces their eardrums! Coming from the female, who screeches incessantly, I find this to be rather hypercritical! Yes the tedium continues, sigh!

Day 543 of Captivity

I have had the most dreadful few days, I have been so ill. I think the kelb must have infected me with his disgusting germs, as it is most suspicious that he was ill at the same time. He is always breathing his foul breath on me; he must have contaminated me. Not only have I been ill, but also I have been ill with a repulsive kelb virus! I could have expired! I have spent much of my time asleep, too weak to engage in much skullduggery.

I was feeling much better last night and decided a spot of skulking was in order, especially as the Infidels have got off lightly these past few days. I managed to entice the male Infidel into following me about for a time, but he soon tired of it and lapsed into a bout of rage! He can be so tiresome! The female wasn't engaging in being a source of my amusement either.

This morning she cooked a huge pan of stew, it smelt so lovely. I did attempt to remove the lid and taste some but she heard me clattering about in the kitchen and dismissed me from the room. They are so selfish and never share their consumables. I have to eat a horrid gruel of raw chicken, while they banquet on all kinds of wonderful things. In order to exact my revenge, I ate the cover from the female Infidel's novel she is reading while they were quaffing! She, who laughs last, laughs longest!

Day 555 of Captivity

The Infidels quaffed down a Chinese take away last night, and despite my best endeavors to look as emaciated and pathetic as possible, the greedy beasts didn't offer me even a morsel! I was infuriated! Being an opportunist, I waited for them to engage in conversation after the meal and before they had chance to clear away the plates. I jumped up at the kitchen table and scoffed down as many scraps as I could, before the evil crone of a female Infidel caught me and sucked the joy out of my life by taking away the plates whilst berating me. The shadow of bore strikes again; she is a nuisance!

She was quite livid last week when I attempted to eat a peasant cat that decided to perch on the windowsill outside the lounge! I think what galled her was the fact that I became ever so slightly entangled in the wooden blinds at the window. It was not my fault, and the intruder needed to be dispatched immediately for displaying such insolent behavior. The female did not seem at all perturbed by the intrusion and was more concerned by the assault on the blinds! She is quite unhinged and I do worry about her at times.

Day 563 of Captivity

The female Infidel was busy cooking dinner in the kitchen this afternoon, and the wizened old shrew would not let me assist. Every time I jumped up at the counter to better see what she was up to, she growled at me and sent me on my way. She grudgingly spared me a carrot to chew on, which I took into the lounge. She was blissfully unaware and thought I was happily chewing on my carrot, and left me to my own devices for a few moments. I took this opportunity to abscond with a string of fairy lights that the female Infidel thinks looks fabulous in a bowl with some pot pourri. I beg to differ and ate the fairy lights and some of the pot pourri as well! I chewed them into several smaller strings, which seemed to incense the female Infidel somewhat. I was sent directly to my crate for some time, apparently for my own safety! Once she released me I shredded the dishcloth. As if a little solitary confinement would bring my reign of evilness to a standstill. I scoff at you Infidels!

Day 571 of Captivity

1 shoe (the female Infidel was a bit put out by this as it was her favorite shoes, ah she still has one so I don't really see what she has to complain about!)
The Infidel's tea as it was left marinating, this made me sick, and they really ought to learn to cook!
I have dug a trench right round the garden, which infuriated the female Infidel, as the soil was wet and I got very dirty, so she bathed me; which in turn infuriated me!
1 kitchen chair leg, I only chewed it, it was not as if I completely destroyed it, but of course there were histrionics from the Infidels
Several dishcloths and tea towels
The new oven gloves
A candle, not too tasty so I spit it out all over the place, and the female became quite vexed, as she had not long done the Hoovering.
2 pens, managed to deposit some of the ink on the carpet before they were confiscated.

All in all, I have had a pretty good week, although the Infidels do not seem to be of the same opinion on the subject. In fact I overheard the female Infidel muttering about taking me to see someone called Vlad the Impaler to have my hormones suppressed, as I am due to be inoculated anyway. I am not too sure I am happy about this, particularly as I heard her say that euthanasia might be cheaper in the long run!

There seems to be no hope of ever enticing my Arabic neighbors into a rescue attempt. They have forsaken me and gone over to the dark side, they are harboring a peasant cat in their accommodation! I have tried to warn them on several occasions that it had got in their home by shouting across at them, but now it seems the peasant has got comfortable and has bewitched them. It is wearing a collar, which usually means that they intend to keep you. I am demoralized; if anything I thought they might be my saviors one day. To add insult to injury the peasant keeps looking smugly across at me from the window of their abode. I am resigned to the fact I am facing more endless days of monotony under the regime of the Infidels.

Day 577 of Captivity

There is no end to the cruelty that these Infidels will stoop to. This weekend I was taken in the motor vehicle to visit the Vet! I do not like the Vet; he generally sticks needles in me for no good reason. I refused to get out of my crate when we arrived and made sure that the female Infidel had to heave and pant to get me out. I then refused to walk on my own; I was not about to make it easy for them. The female seems to believe I settle better with her, so she had the job of carrying me in and up the 2 flights of stairs. She was wheezing like an asthmatic Rhino by the time we arrived at the desk of the Vet, most undignified!

The Vet then stabbed me in the neck, not once, but three times! It was most disagreeable and if I could have turned my head I would have bitten him. The one thing I did like about the Vet's was that there were many peasant cats just there for the taking, although of course the shadow of bore did not allow me to indulge in any such delight. She really does suck the fun out of everything! I was made to stand about while the Infidels prattled on with the Vet. Finally they decided to return to the motor vehicle. I walked there on my own, I was only too happy to be retreating from the Vet's.

We set off for home again. Just as we were turning onto the street where we reside, I exacted my revenge. I vomited through the bars of the crate, managing to catch the female Infidel as it passed through the bars of the crate, splashing onto her face, which was aghast. The look of horror was truly priceless! An appropriate reprisal I feel.

Day 579 of Captivity

Today has been such a drag. A most heinous dust storm swept through Riyadh this afternoon, turning the sky almost red! We were confined to the prison, but quite frankly you wouldn't have got me outside today for anything! I have spent much of the day lounging on the couch, in a state of unconsciousness.

In an attempt to alleviate my boredom I went to forage for food, as I was close to starvation given that the miserly Infidels did not share their dinner with me just for a change. It smelt so nice and I gave them my best "wasting away" stare too! I really don't know how they managed to resist; they are so insensitive.

The female Infidel made some shortbread this morning, which took my fancy. It was on the kitchen counter under a huge plastic dome. I was so annoyed; I had just managed to get the dome off and removed a large slice for myself. As I was about to clamp my jaws shut around my ill-gotten gains that infuriating cretin of a male Infidel caught me in the act and swiped my contraband. I was crushed. He then banished me to my cell, berating me all the way. I am waiting to be released for a second attempt, as I think I would have quite enjoyed eating that! Damn Infidels!

Day 597 of Captivity

Those dastardly villains have really gone too far this time. I have a cut on my leg, which I have been keeping clean by chewing it. This does not meet with the standards of the female Infidel, however, and she has put some horrid stingy stuff on it and taped it all up. To add to my humiliation she has then forced me to wear a stupid sock, to apparently keep it clean. I think she just wants me to look a fool. She is very cruel and told me if she catches me chewing the sock, she will put Olbas oil on it to put me off! She is a scoundrel and her cruelty knows no bounds! She is convincing herself it is for my own good. Poor deluded imbecile!

Not only have I had to endure this intolerable cruelty, but also I was then forced to parade through the streets this morning, looking like I had a wooden leg. Of course I milked it for all it was worth, and when we passed anyone I put on my most pathetic of faces. I did get some sympathy, but no one seems to have felt compelled to come to my aid and free me. I am still a captive. I have concluded that all the Infidels must be as depraved as each other. I continue to document their acts of sadism against me, in the vain hope that someone out there will take pity on me and come to my rescue. In the meantime I remain in this soul-destroying existence. The Kelb is drooling on the couch next to me; he really is repugnant.

The Infidels managed to compound their abuse a few weeks back, thinking that I would be willing to share a chaise with the kelb for the evening whilst they slept. Most kind of them to free me from my cell, but really, sleep with the kelb? I choose jail! I skulked off to my cell in a sullen mood. I am a Pure bred Arabian princess and he is a disgusting troll, I would rather be flayed alive and rolled in salt than have to endure his drooling, smelly carcass next to me all evening. The very thought makes my blood run cold! Will this persecution ever end?

Day 599 of Captivity

The female Infidel woke the male with a cup of tea and some toast this morning. She then went back downstairs to get her own, leaving the kelb and I in the room with the male Infidel. I was lolling about on the Infidel's bed, when suddenly I lunged at the male and absconded with a slice of his toast smothered in delicious peanut butter. The male was infuriated by my impudence and he jumped up out of bed and began pursuing me most vigorously. We danced from one side of the bed to the other, and I could see he was about to explode with fury. The female Infidel was aghast, as she opened the door to witness a naked male Infidel lunging across the bed like Superman making a grab for my retreating posterior as I made a run for the now open door. I am not sure who was more disturbed by the vision of a naked male Infidel leaping through the air in a pathetic attempt to catch me, myself or the female Infidel. She looked quite pale.

I made my way to the mid landing and relished my spoils. The male Infidel sulked for quite some time, he did not even crack when I leant against him with huge sad eyes, fluttering my eyelashes. That usually gets him every time, he is such a drama queen, he would have given me the toast anyway, I just couldn't wait! The kelb was horrified and kept giving me withering stares from his bed, letting me know that he found my behavior distasteful. He then had the audacity to make several advances on my person throughout the day, when will he realize that I would never stoop so low!

The female Infidel spent the morning baking the most delicious chocolate muffins, which she put under that annoying dome to prevent me from partaking in what should have been my share. She is so miserly, her excuse is that chocolate is bad for dogs, looking at what it has done to her ass, perhaps she is right!

Day 601 of Captivity

The female Infidel was ill yesterday. She went to bed to wallow in her own self pity and of course the creepy kelb went with her to lie by her side, throwing her the odd pitying look and being a general crawler. He disgusts me! I went up there too, because I am quite nosey. The female Infidel eventually drifted off to sleep, but lying watching her being feeble was becoming rather tedious. I was bored and decided to sprint round the room at top speed, jumping hard onto the bed a couple of times, until the female Infidel sat up wide eyed and swearing like a Trooper, flapping her arms around and generally looking outraged. She then threw the bedroom door open and dismissed me, sending me from the room. I was only too glad to leave and went downstairs; her reddened distorted face and shrill ranting retreating into the distance as I ran downstairs to the safety of the male Infidel, who at least saw the funny side to my escapade. She has no sense of fun!

It is raining again today, and there is no chance the female will get me out there running. I hate rain! I am so bored though. The Infidels will not allow me to amuse myself by sprinting round the lounge. I have thrown the couch into the window a couple of times, which is enough to send the female Infidel into a rage, she keeps threatening to crate me if I don't calm down. I have indulged in a spot of counter surfing, but the stingy Infidels have taken to hiding any contraband in the microwave and I can't quite get the door open myself. I have tried dragging it off the counter to see if the fall would open the door, but the noise it makes tends to alert the Infidels who are never too far away from me for some strange reason.

I am lying on the back of the couch staring out of the windows, amusing myself by barking at passers by, this activity tends to gall the Infidels, especially when the vacuous kelb joins in, because he is very loud and irritating. And of course he never used to bark until I came along! No wonder they captured me, he must have bored them to tears!

Day 618 of Captivity

The other night the Infidels were feeling lazy and ordered their dinner from the restaurant. The male Infidel put some money on the dresser ready to pay for the delivery and then popped to the lavatory. While he was gone, I surreptitiously removed the money from the dresser and took it into the lounge and shredded it into a million pieces. The male returned from the lavatory and sat on the couch waiting for the food to arrive. I lay on the couch with a sly grin on my face. The doorbell rang and I have to admit to taking some perverse pleasure out of seeing him go to the dresser, see the money was missing, then go about the house shouting to everyone asking them if they had removed it. The look of sheer horror as he passed through the lounge and saw the carpet festooned with confetti of money was just hilarious. Not nearly as funny as seeing him red faced on the door step explaining to the restaurant that he would have to pass by later and drop off some money, as his beloved pet had ingested the money he had set aside. More amusing was the sheer realization that it was one puzzle he was not going to ever be able to reconstruct as I had swallowed the odd piece.

I am suffering for my deed now as a few nights ago the house was invaded by yet more Infidels. These are the very Infidels that spawned the female! They are sleeping in the house and still have not left; it has been almost a week now. I hope that they are not staying for good. The Infidel they call Granddad worries me. I urinated on the end of his bed to let him know that his trespassing did not amuse me. I have tried to gain access to the room since, but they seem to be keeping it locked up tight.

Day 623 of Captivity

What an absolutely dreadful week I have had! Not only have I had to endure having more Infidels around me, but I have also been having another pseudo season. The kelb has been a dribbling, whining buffoon, no change from normal granted, but he has followed my every move and been fawning all over me. I have standards! I was taken to the Vet to see if they can help, as this has been the worst one in a long time. The Infidels have found a new Vet and seemed to be very confident in him. There was talk of x-rays to confirm possible tissue remnant and possibly another spay operation! I feel pretty fed up at the moment and I swear if the kelb doesn't stop his whining, I will bite his face off!

On the bright side, there was a glimmer of hope yesterday! I saw a peasant cat on our bike ride and one tug, I managed to snap my leash and break free. I was so excited at the prospect of dispatching the cat; I didn't realize I could have run away! I ran off at top speed and screeched to an emergency stop just over the peasant creature, but it made off and ran under a car. The female Infidel was frantic and screaming my name. She released the kelb from the bike to chase me down. The cat ran under the nearest car and I stood guard ready to pounce when it came out, but unfortunately I was so focused on the cat, I didn't see the female coming and she grabbed my collar and walked the kelb and I home. She was in a black mood. When she got home, she realized I was bleeding; I had skinned my pads and the back of my rear leg in my emergency skid on the concrete. She has put some cream on them and will not let me keep them clean. When I chew them clean, she threatens to make me wear a lampshade on my head, these Infidels are just the pits!

We did not go out on the bike this morning, but were walked round. I will wait until next time and run away, that vacuous cat distracted me, but now I know there is a way...........

Day 640 of Captivity

I have been violated! Those devils took me into town today and left me at the Vets. I was then sawn in half and gutted like a fish! I am now languishing on the couch minutes from death. The female Infidel clearly feels guilty for her part in this, she has been flapping round and giving me drinks of water. The kelb keeps pushing his fat face close to mine and licking me! If he gets close enough I will bite him, this is his entire fault! I am taking solace in the fact that, little does he know, but he is next and they are taking his man bits. After all the surgery I went through there were no tissue stumps or ectopic tumors to be found, therefore it must be a hormone imbalance. The kelb has to go in for an operation as a result, every cloud! He will be barking castrato as of Sunday. I would sneer at him, but I am in too much pain! I feel I must milk this for the full duration. Those scoundrels will suffer for this!

On the bright side the grey-haired Infidels have gone back from whence they came. I didn't manage to eat much of their stuff, as the shadow of bore was never far away. I only managed a quick nibble on some headphones and a book. The kelb and I certainly seemed to cause the elderly ones great stress while they were visiting. They offered to care for the kelb and I and the adolescent Infidels so that the male and female Infidel could languish in a hotel in Marrakech for a few days, having abandoned us to enjoy a break. Don't worry we made the decrepit Infidels suffer! The kelb kept trying to make me his woman during my pseudo season, a hypothesis so grisly, bile rises up in my mouth at the very thought! When the Infidels returned from their jaunt, the elderly Infidels were rocking in a corner, truly scarred from the stress of coping with my pseudo season. I think it will be several years before they ever manage to convince them to look after us again!

The female kindly brought me back two sheep's leather pouffes from her voyage, which I am delighted with and have distressed a little.

I will write more if I survive the night and gain my strength back. *peffle*

Day 641 of Captivity

I just about made it through the night! I felt very uncomfortable and shuffled about a bit, the female thought it was my wound and allowed me to get comfy. I urinated on her couch. The male Infidel was none too pleased, but the female, still wracked with guilt defended me saying that I was probably still a bit out of it on the general anesthetic. Little does she know that had the male not taken me to the garden and I was able to push I would have defecated on there as well! I finally managed to do that in the garden, after the humiliation of having wet cloths to assist me. Is there no end to the degradation I must endure!

The Infidels are clearly beside themselves with guilt for having me maimed. They actually allowed me to languish on their bed all night in between them. I woke in the night a couple of times and was very sick. The female was alerted to it and took me out the back. I woke her this morning chewing on my stitches and she has now dressed me in a disgusting Adidas T shirt and tied a ribbon round the waist in an attempt to stop me. Adidas! I am Gucci or Amani for goodness sake! Not only have they injured me but they are now humiliating me as well. The female's guilt has obviously eroded as she has chastised me several times this morning for chewing my stitches. She clearly underestimates the power of the Saluki when it comes to sulking, she will pay dearly for this!

I can hardly wait until it is the turn of the kelb; he is trotting about with an air of smug satisfaction. *Growl*

Day 643 of Captivity

The cruelty of the Infidels knows no bounds! Not satisfied with having me sawn in half, they have now attached a hideous plastic lampshade to my collar. It is like an albatross around my neck. What kind of sadists are they? I have taken to my cell, as I am too ashamed to be seen in public looking like Shakespeare's dog! It is useful though, for knocking their precious things off tables and chaffing the kelb's posterior! The bonus is that the kelb is afraid of the collar, so I keep looming at him. It is most amusing seeing the vapid creature completely freak out!

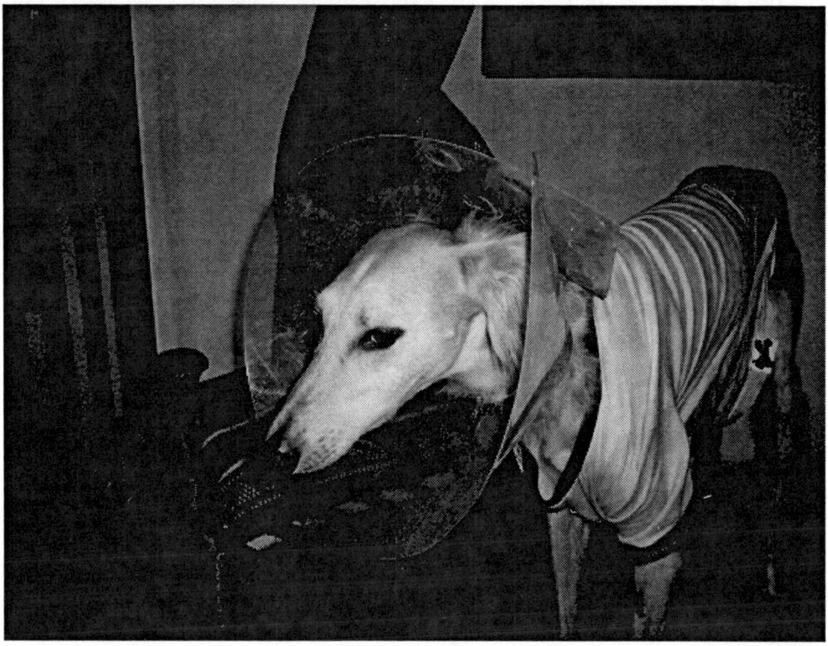

O' frabjous day! Callooh! Callay! The kelb bids farewell to his plums tomorrow. Whilst I can't reach my own stitches I am sure I will manage to gnaw on his! *Smiles smugly*

Day 645 of Captivity

Not satisfied with having me gutted, those depraved Infidels have gone on a mutilation spree and have now taken the kelb to the Vet! He came back looking like Ricky Hatton had used his scrotum as a punch bag! He is not amused and has been rather pathetic. I was sawn in half and you don't see me rolling around being feeble! I have taken the bull by the horns and managed to work out how to push past that lampshade and get to my stitches. However, those cursed Infidels have discovered my little secret and have taken the torture up a level. I am now wandering about with a satellite dish on my head picking up Al Jazeera and sulking like only a Saluki can. The lampshade I am currently wearing would be more at home at Jodrell Bank!

They have also discovered that I have been scratching my chest and got it very raw. In an attempt to prevent this I am wearing stupid socks and a hideous off cast T-shirt, the hand me down of a sweaty adolescent! It smells strange and belongs in Barry Manilow's wardrobe. The smell can only be described as youth. I am now confined to throwing myself about in my crate, writhing in agony and unable to chew my stitches. Can life be any more desolate?

Day 649 of Captivity

The Infidels thought the war was won when they put that huge cone on my head, but they underestimated me. Just before they were going to bed the other night I chucked myself about and managed to smash the cone in half and get free of it. It was very late at night, so the Infidels did a repair job on it and then the female guarded me all night. The following morning she called that evil Vet and made arrangements to take me back! She seemed very worried and had been crying in the night. Clearly the guilt is back.

That afternoon they returned me to the Vet. There was a lot of wringing of hands and worried expressions. It was discovered that I had removed all of my stitches and done some damage to the tissue underneath. I had an infection and was quite poorly. The Vet gave me an injection in my back; the needle was huge! Neither of the Infidels could watch, but they didn't stop him either. They then took me back to the car and on the way home they bought a new giant lampshade to put on my head. As if the trip to the Vet had not been torturous enough! To let them know how much I objected I vomited all over the female Infidel just minutes from home. I thought she was going to cry; she was literally covered in it.

It seems that dastardly Vet had given the Infidels some tablets for me to sedate me and keep me from getting at my wound for a few days. The female gave me 2 tablets and stayed up with me all night, as I fought it and would not settle. Eventually I calmed down and the Infidels have kept me in that state for a few days now. They have slept by my side taking it in turns to watch over me and brought me drinks of water, and fed me and just made sure I was well. Perhaps I have misjudged these Infidels, although I suspect a more likely explanation is that they have not been giving me sedatives at all, but mind-altering drugs in an attempt to trick me into liking them. I am sure once I am lucid again I will see things more clearly.

In an attempt to make up for their evil deeds the Infidels went out yesterday and bought me a new chair to sleep in. It hardly compensates for having me sawn in half, but it will do for a start!

I am now being as annoying as possible whining in my highest voice and digging up the couch. When I am well again, I have a lot of making up to do.

Day 656 of Captivity

During the dark days of my illness I flicked through some of the Infidel's novels. It would appear that Infidels take a perverse pleasure in torturing royalty. They had such titles as "The Man in the Iron Mask". What devils have held me captive? I have set aside Machiavelli's "The Prince" for future perusal. I suspect I might enjoy that title.

The Infidels have finally removed the cone of anguish that they had burdened me with these past few weeks. I note that they have kept it and renamed it the cone of coercion. It is in the back room glinting at me fiendishly. As soon as the opportunity arises I will eat it.

I am slightly sad to see the cone go, as I had developed a great game for torturing the kelb. I would stand over him with the cone and trap his face in it. If you saw his eyes bulge and his legs flail you would think it was vacuum-sealed. Most amusing! I also quite enjoyed using it as a weapon of mass destruction and knee capping the Infidels with it. That said I am fully functioning again as counter surfing champion KSA; the cone was somewhat hindering.

The female Infidel bathed me this morning and then dragged her Victorian torture tool known as the" Furminator" through my coat. I was just pleased to be free of the cone of anguish so I did not put up a fight. The kelb was bathed too.

The Infidels were preparing their dinner. In their absence I chewed two enormous holes in one of the throws on the couch. It has been ages since I have been able to wreck havoc on their lives and I didn't want them forgetting just what I am capable of did I?

Day 664 of Captivity

Following the ups and downs of my illness, life has returned to the dull monotony of Infidel hell that I previously existed in. To pass the time I have been perusing the Infidel's vast DVD collection. I came across an interesting series called "Prison Break", however I am not prepared to have a map of the prison tattooed onto my royal coat and I certainly don't want the kelb getting in on the plan! He is far too vapid and his foul stench would give the game away.

I have taken to wandering nocturnally round the bedroom, occasionally bursting into song of such ear splitting pitch it would stun a thrush in mid flight. This normally rouses the female Infidel. I have to say she is a philistine where my singing is concerned. Waking in the night brings out the shrew in her and she is prone to fits of apoplexy.

To compensate for my nocturnal activity, I am prone to narcolepsy once I have assured she is awake and mobile. I tend to spend the day languishing on the couch, shouting abuse at the occasional passing peasant, whilst the female Infidel scowls menacingly from the opposite side of the room with her moronic sidekick drooling at her feet.

I have set aside "The Great Escape" and "Escape From Alcatraz" for future viewing, as "Prison Break" was rather disappointing. Tattoos! *Shudder*

Day 665 of Captivity

I am outraged! The female Infidel maimed me with her cycling contraption this morning. The foul kelb stopped to evacuate his bowels and the female Infidel was most put out that I was attempting to alert her to a peasant cat encroaching on our personal space. The sheer impudence of the grimy creature was inconceivable! The female Infidel was attempting to pick up the kelb's leavings (a ghastly activity these Infidels perform that I have found most peculiar!) She became quite cross as I attempted to pull the cycling contraption round so that I could dispatch the ghastly peasant cat. She attempted to mount the cycling contraption and ignore the brute. I jumped up and scratched her arm to bring her out of the stupor she was clearly in. She became more determined to cycle on, there was nothing for it; I threw myself against the rear tire in an attempt to stop the madness. She cursed loudly and told me to stop being such an imbecile. I am now sporting a large friction burn on my chest and a severe reprimand from the female Infidel for allegedly attempting to take her life. She can be such a drama queen! When I licked off all of the iodine and antiseptic cream, she even had the gall to threaten me with the cone of despair! The abuse continues.

The kelb was supposed to be taken to the Vet yesterday evening to have his boosters. He managed to get a reprieve, as when the male Infidel came home from work he said he was far too tired for such ventures! From what I can gather his occupation entails his sitting in a large leather chair in a big office, I cannot understand how that would be very tiring at all. I am pretty sure by the look on the female Infidel's face that she was struggling to comprehend this too. She muttered something about being slightly put out she was unable to drive herself. At least I think that is what the cursing meant.

Day 667 of Captivity

The vacuous kelb ate some red ants yesterday whilst inhaling his supper. It has amused me no end, as he looks like a canine Mick Jagger! His lips swelled right up making his head look even fatter than usual. He has not had a good day, he was given his boosters yesterday in his back legs, and so to top it off he has been walking as if the Vet left the thermometer in. From the front he looks like Mick Jagger and from the rear he looks like John Inman. He has been such a bore and just lay around feeling sorry for himself. I have been forced to find my own amusement. I spent the morning distressing the Infidel's camel stool and pulling out wadding from the storage in the back room and shredding it leaving a trail of destruction for the female Infidel to tut over.

The male Infidel cooked this evening. As they were loading up the dishwasher I did a pre-wash, I do like to do my bit. I think the male needs to tweak his recipe, it made my tongue burn and my eyes water! It has put me off assisting them for a time. No doubt I shall be spending tomorrow licking my anus like a common kelb! Damn his ham-fisted use of curry powder!

Day 670 of Captivity

The Infidels went out last night to partake in an evening of drunken debauchery at an undisclosed location. They are truly scandalous and came home in the early hours of the morning in a drunken stupor; they are such heathens. I have my suspicions that they may have eaten prohibited pig meat as well, they are just depraved enough!

Before they went out they spent ages primping themselves. While the female Infidel was in the shower she left the clothes she was to wear out ready and her new shoes. I have not eaten a pair of shoes in a while and thought this a good opportunity to revisit the pleasure. I managed to chew a small hole in the side of one of her shoes while she was busy in the bathroom. She became quite enraged when she came out of the bathroom and caught me just about to have a chew on the heels, I have never seen her move so quickly and the language was atrocious!

Needless to say the Infidels have spent much of the day in bed. I tried to rouse them to let me out, but it was a pointless exercise. I was left aghast when I wrapped myself up in the kilim and began chewing on the corners, the female Infidel suddenly developed the hearing of a fruit bat and she was out of bed quicker than a flash and issuing death threats. She trudged down to the garden with me and became very impatient as I plodded round the beds smelling the flowers and taking my time to enjoy the baking sun, which seemed to turn the female Infidel an ashen shade. They have not moved much today and look like death warmed up, the only thing that gets them active is playfully jumping on their heads, they don't seem too pleased about it either!

Day 672 of Captivity

Yesterday was the hairy Infidel's birthday. The ungrateful young upstart didn't seem to appreciate my gift of warm chicken vomit that I unselfishly left on his pillow for him. He thundered down the stairs bellowing like a bull and he called me some very unkind names! The youth of today are just so ungrateful. Next time I shall defecate in his slippers!

This morning the female Infidel went on a jaunt to a coffee morning on another compound, where she quaffed cakes (as if her ass isn't big enough!) and sat about all morning twittering on to any poor soul she could detain. I can just imagine the anguish, those poor people! The female Infidel didn't even bring back a morsel for us, the greedy wench! The kelb and I were left in the care of the hairy Infidel and the sullen nerdy Infidel. I am still sulking about the hairy one's churlish behavior yesterday. To teach him a lesson, I decided I *would* defecate in his slippers! My generosity knows no bounds. By the smell of them, I wasn't the first, although I couldn't name the breed from the stench, possibly Orangutan or some form of marsupial. I am dozing on the couch awaiting the fallout when he discovers them.

Day 679 of Captivity

Words fail me; I have been subjected to the most intolerable cruelty. The greedy fat male Infidel has just sat and eaten an entire bag of Maltesers, and despite my most pitiful looks, he didn't even spare me a crumb! I am outraged. I am considering chewing his notes during his next visit to the kitchen, he is working hard on his note taking for his Masters, I am sure eating every other page would be due recompense for his miserly behavior!

They had a stir-fry for tea and all I managed to procure was one measly bean sprout. I wouldn't mind, but the corpulent kelb ate that!

I am still sulking with the kelb after his stupidity last night! The female Infidel actually allowed us to have a rawhide chew each last night. It has been some time since we had one, because the kelb always spoils things. I hid mine upstairs on the landing so they would think I had eaten it, then I taunted the kelb hoping to entice him into giving his up, but he was not giving in easily and he ignored me! I became tired of him; he does tend to bring on a feeling of malaise after just a few moments in his irksome company.

The little sneak sidled out of the room, as soon as my back was turned, and went upstairs to retrieve the chew I had hidden. He skipped smugly into the room with one sticking out of each side of his vacuous great mouth. He even had the audacity to gallop round the room dancing with glee and taunting me. Needless to say I was extremely vexed and I let him have it. The female Infidel chastised ME and then confiscated the chews. I berated the kelb for some time after they were taken and pouted at him from the couch across the room, whilst he sat gazing vacantly in the direction that the chews were last seen. I could almost hear the air rushing around the emptiness that is his skull. He sucks the fun right out of life!

Day 680 of Captivity

The miserly Infidels have only fed me once today, claiming that because I vomited a little it was for my own good! Faint with hunger I was forced to find my own sustenance. I managed to intercept a cockroach and was just about to ingest it when all hell broke lose and there was a lot of shrieking and flapping of arms and wringing of hands. I thought the hairy one was going to soil his trousers! My meal was confiscated and freed (stupid Buddhists!) much to my disgust; even Papillion was allowed to eat the cockroaches.

Imagine my glee when I learned that roast beef with all the trimmings was on the Infidel's menu this evening. I should have known the hedonistic, potbellied simians would eat it all themselves! However, intelligence sources have confirmed that the hairy one and the strange nerdy one are off to the dentist tomorrow; hopefully their mandibles will be wired shut, leaving an opening for my counter surfing deftness! Should I not perish from lack of nutrients in the night, I am reduced to chewing my own feet and the occasional nibble of the camel stool! How the kelb survives with his body mass I do not know!

Day 682 of Captivity

The female Infidel is still sulking because yesterday she had a couple of visitors. I was already hyper before they arrived and had been performing the wall of death, much to the female Infidel's horror and she rushed about the villa grabbing precious things whilst berating me. This only made the game so much more fun and sent me into a state of euphoria. I was in the middle of a lap of the villa when the visitors arrived. I felt it only good manners to rush to greet them and I took a good run up and launched myself into one of them, a small elderly lady. The female Infidel then lost the plot and banished me to my crate. How was I to know I could have broken her hip, I was just being a good host!

Needless to say I have had to endure the most intolerable level of pouting today, and they say Salukis can sulk! I have spent the day sleeping off the tedium of her bad temper.

Day 685 of Captivity

The female Infidel fed us very late this morning, because instead of catering to our every desire, she spent the morning on the phone twittering on to some poor undeserving soul. I can only imagine they were on the other end of the line sticking forks in their necks and slamming their heads repeatedly in the freezer, I know I wished I was! FINALLY the poor victim must have made their excuses and escaped, and the gabbling fool got off the phone.

After she fed us, to illustrate my displeasure at having to wait, I regurgitated the entire meal up onto the carpet in the lounge. I would have liked to be able to vomit through the blinds, but I am still practicing my projectile technique. The repugnant kelb hearing the commotion came to investigate. At this point the female Infidel became enraged and started roaring at us both to get out, flailing her arms at us, like a spit fire plummeting to Earth!

I took an enormous amount of satisfaction in seeing the kelb out maneuver her in the dining room and make a run for it back into the lounge. Once he got there he gobbled up the pile of steaming spew, whilst I roared with laughter from the safety of the kitchen. I really thought the female Infidel would have a stroke, as she began venting her spleen. Yes, the kelb is not so adorable now is he missy!

Day 692 of Captivity

I actually reduced the strange nerdy Infidel to a sniveling heap yesterday afternoon. He had a small memory card in his pocket and just before he went to the bathroom he dropped it onto the floor. I was going to alert him, but thought it would be much more pleasurable to chew it to tiny fragments. I was right; it was indeed pleasurable and made more so when he realized and burst into tears. I felt utter jubilation when the female Infidel then berated not me, but the nerdy one, for having left it lying about, because after all he should know what I am like. I lay on the sofa opposite and smirked at him as he sat sullenly throwing me the odd surly look. I thought the nerdy one would implode, as I moved over to him and lay my head on his lap, smirking up at him. He looked positively wretched!

It was a different story this morning when I stole an English muffin from the back of the kitchen counter and ate it. The male Infidel raged at me, something about having to drive 8 hours just to get them. Perhaps they shouldn't have been so reckless with their valuables in future; after all they know what I am like! I believe the nerdy one felt vindicated, a small sacrifice on my part.

Day 693 of Captivity

This morning I was subjected to a most barbaric attack from the bellicose kelb! I was in the lounge when I heard an insolent fowl goading me from the garden. I at once leapt into the affray and took off running, only to be squashed by the corpulent kelb in his headlong lurch towards the door. The churlish creature jostled past me and I was flung unceremoniously into the refuse receptacle, at which point I landed hard and almost shattered my spine!

I shrieked in agony and when no one came to my assistance, was forced to drag my battered frame back into the lounge. I held up my disfigured leg, so the female Infidel could know that her toady had physically crippled me. She made a contemptible effort to placate me, but I was overwrought and took to my crate for the rest of the morning. I shall seek retribution once I regain the strength in my withered limb. I have spent the afternoon chewing my nails into sharp points, which I shall insert into the kelb's ears until he cries. Vengeance shall be mine!

Day 705 of Captivity

The tedium of living with these wretched Infidels continues to bore me to tears. I have been so consumed with languor; I decided to entertain myself with a spot of singing this evening. This seemed to gall the Infidels as they were trying to watch Star Trek at the time. A story about a fat elderly man who resides on a space ship and apparently females are powerless to resist his geriatric charms. It is a very dated movie anyway and my singing is much more engaging. I had to sing very loud to drown out the surround sound in their movie machine, but I am proud to say I reached some notes I didn't know were possible. The boorish Infidels of course did not appreciate my musical talents and insinuated that they would rather gouge at their ears with a cheese grater and rub their tattered remains with lemons than listen to another note!

Yesterday I had to suffer the indignity of being bundled into my crate for several hours, whilst the voracious Infidels went out to a restaurant to stuff their porcine faces! I tormented the kelb by singing tribal songs of my youth to him for two hours. He seemed absolutely delighted to see the Infidels on their return and when they released me from my cell the malodorous creature attempted to bite my face off! I almost fainted from the stench of his fetid breath and had to wash my face several times to remove his putrid stench from my coat. It was truly ghastly!

The male Infidel gave us a small amount of chicken this afternoon, his idea of a little snack. On inspection I made the grisly discovery that he had attempted to feed me a chicken's derriere! I didn't even protest when the greedy kelb pilfered my portion, and took a great amount of satisfaction in watching the half-witted creature scoff it down as if it were the best caviar. He truly is an imbecile and the male Infidel is a scoundrel!

I shall continue with my singing later when the Infidels attempt to retire for the evening, I am sure they will appreciate my dulcet tones. That will teach them to try and poison me with a chicken's bum! Royalty does not chew on the toilet parts of animals, unlike dissolute kelbs!

Day 706 of Captivity

I soon tired of attempting to entertain the uncultured Infidels last evening and decided that a snooze would shut out their monotonous prattle. I fell asleep on the couch and lapsed into a deep slumber. The goon of a male Infidel struck the fear of Allah into me, when he apparently sneezed and blew away the inhabitants of the neighboring town! I sat bolt upright and in my state of panic I was forced to hurl myself at the nerdy Infidel who was presumptuous enough to be sat next to me on the couch.

I landed in his face and because of his puny frame, he buckled under the force of me catapulting into him and his glasses flew off. I eventually managed to gain a foothold on his capacious head and I scrabbled on to freedom, leaving the jelly-headed youth gibbering on the couch, whilst the Infidels collapsed in peals of laughter at his predicament. They are as cruel to their young as they are to their captives. I actually felt sympathy for him for a fleeting moment, but the feeling passed as I spotted my favorite ball on the carpet.

Day 708 of Captivity

The female Infidel was throwing herself about on the running machine this morning. For a brief moment, I did consider that it might be an enjoyable diversion to jump onto the machine whilst she was wheezing and sweating away like a rasping old hippo. On further consideration I decided against such action, one miscalculation on my part and her gargantuan carcass could have crushed me! Not quite how I pictured my glorious exit to this world!

This afternoon I dragged out the battered remains of the TV control that was stupidly abandoned in between the cushions of the couch. I was just about to disassemble it to finally discover what is inside when the female Infidel discovered me and put an end to that plan. I was so miffed; I ate her tour guide of Istanbul with gay abandon, while she went to the lavatory. Ha! That will put an end to any plot she might be hatching to swan off and enjoy herself! Find the Blue Mosque now with half a map, not that they would let you in anyway you stinky Infidel!

Day 712 of Captivity

I was so dreadfully ill in the night on Wednesday and woke the female Infidel in the early hours. I think the kelb might have tried to have me dispatched; perhaps it would be prudent of me to employ a food taster in future. The neighbor's peasant cat might be a good candidate although I am not sure I trust those princes of darkness with my royal constitution! I had to wake the female Infidel 3 times to tend to me, she was in a black mood, as the male Infidel seemingly slept through the entire episode, yet when she asked him whether he would like a cup of tea and some breakfast, he suddenly developed the hearing of a fruit bat. I thought the female Infidel would implode, but she took out her frustration on the crockery.

The female Infidel thinks that my bout of illness was down to my greediness! How VERY dare she! I am the very epitome of restraint, unlike her toady; he is a walking garbage disposal unit. I was crushed by her accusations and sulked on the couch all morning.

This morning ravaged with hunger, having only had a light meal yesterday I was forced to stoop to counter surfing in the kitchen. This resulted in the nerdy Infidel being chastised for not completing his chores and he was berated and forced to sort out the dishes. A small recompense for having my food source whisked away. The bonus was the nerdy one sulked and was miserable, I always get a degree of gratification out of seeing him suffer.

Day 715 of Captivity

The Infidel's barbarism knows no bounds! Today I have been feeling rather energetic and spent the morning carrying out vigorous exercises in order to prevent the onset of heart disease. The female Infidel, however, did not seem amused by my acrobatic endeavors, especially as they threatened to dislodge her precious things or tat as I prefer to refer to it. She was particularly displeased when the kelb joined in, throwing his porcine body around the villa with clear disregard to life or property. However, she too joined in careening about the villa attempting to rescue her tatty belongings from imminent destruction, all to the blood-curdling sound of "The Pogues". Needless to say I ended up in solitary confinement, with her scowling at me from across the room.

The one highlight to the morning was when the AC repairman showed up. The kelb, still delirious from our energetic morning, attempted to run off with his cloth and tools. The poor man was clearly traumatized being faced with such a hideous slathering gargoyle and the kelb received a scruffing for his impudence from the female. The female Infidel blamed me for inciting a riot! I am scandalized, this further added to the time I had to spend in confinement.

I was finally released, but having endured the tedium of what seemed like an eternity in solitary I still felt psyched. When the Infidels sat down to gorge themselves as is there wont, I thought it a good time to alert them to the fact there were interlopers in the street. This seemed to tip the female Infidel over the edge and she returned me to the confines of my crate stating that she would like to eat one meal this week in peace and quiet. It was most amusing when she returned to the kitchen and slipped in some of the kelb's drool and almost split in half. I burst out laughing when she shot across the kitchen, landing hard on her back, winding herself and developing the onset of Tourettes. The kelb beat a hasty retreat.

My goodness, Allah is swift and sure these days!

Day 720 of Captivity

The nerdy Infidel has obviously been biding his time after I recently accosted him. I was sound asleep today on the couch after my morning exercise and he thought it would be amusing to come up behind me and clap loudly. Needless to say I almost suffered a coronary! Not willing to let the little pipsqueak get away with such a brutal assault on my Royal person, I let out a blood-curdling scream. Thinking I was being killed the female Infidel rushed to my aid and the little upstart got a short sharp shrift for behaving like a miscreant. I smirked smugly at him as he beat a retreat, I could still hear his indignant bleating, as the female Infidel berated him further for being argumentative. How I relished my victory!

It was a short lived triumph, however, when I found myself on the receiving end of the harpy just moments later when the little sneak sang like a canary and told the female Infidel that I was distressing the camel stool on the landing. The Infidels just will not be told that it is more authentic if it has Saluki engravings on it. They are so boorish!

Day 728 of Captivity

The holy month of Ramadan is once more on the horizon. Sadly, I must spend it in the company of the proles I reside with instead of with my Bedouin kin. On the up side, the kelb has become more rotund than ever following his castration. He has been placed on a diet, which presents many opportunities for me to persecute him, as he is not amused. His rations have been cut in half, and his face was a picture when he was presented with this meager portion this morning. I decided to wander about the garden until he had eaten, and then very slowly savored every mouthful of my food, while he looked on gormless and drooling. He really is living proof that the male brain resides in the testicles, he is even more vapid than ever since his surgery! He spent 45 minutes licking the ground after we had eaten, in the vain hope of extracting one last morsel from the concrete. Finally, the female Infidel curtly called her beloved toady inside, having had enough of his incessant licking of the concrete. He then had to consume gallons of water, as his mouth must have been dry as a bone! He really is such a nincompoop!

Continuing my torment of the kelb, I vomited this afternoon, but the female Infidel was too quick for me and she managed to sweep me out of the lounge, sparing her carpet. Even more impressive was the fact that she also swept the kelb along with us preventing him from snacking on my leavings and he was forced to look sadly on from behind the locked screen door, as the female Infidel cleaned up the potential meal. He looked crushed making the purge worthwhile.

The female Infidel seems to be under the impression that she is off on a holiday soon. I am outraged that she would consider jetting off to enjoy herself, leaving me behind! I have made several attempts to sabotage her evil plan, but she seems undaunted by them. When I chewed her guidebook, she simply went on line to investigate the place she plans on visiting. I see I shall have to play hardball and eat her laptop or at least chew the cable. She seems to be becoming impervious to my actions of late, very disconcerting!

A couple of days ago whilst out exercising there were two members of the National Guard by the gate. We were on foot as the female Infidel has damaged the rear tire of the cycling contraption.

The National Guard beckoned us, but being virtuous, I ignored them, secretly hoping that seeing I was a prisoner of Infidels; they were going to snatch me and free me. Of course the brazen female went over to engage in conversation with these strange men! I was horrified to discover, it was the kelb they expressed an interest in! They were rather taken with his intimidating physique! One of them even touched his grotesque frame and no doubt had to spend the remains of the day dousing himself in disinfectant! My, times are changing; I never thought I would see the day when a fellow countryman would rather touch a putrid kelb!

Day 734 of Captivity

The female Infidel deigned to cook tea this afternoon. While she was occupied I took the opportunity to gnaw at the zip on one of the sofa cushions. Realizing I had been silent for a time, the old hag came to investigate. She was furious that I had chewed the zip and chased me out of the room, flailing her arms around like a demonic Morris Dancer and bellowing like a cow in labor. She then started fussing over the cushions. An opportune moment presented itself for me to meander into the kitchen and consume around 200g of butter that was left carelessly unattended. The look of horror and the realization that this oversight on her part would come back and haunt her later this evening or even better in the early hours of the morning, was just priceless! I have tummy ache and foresee vomit or a canine pooh pancake in her future. She does not seem happy sitting next to me on the sofa as my stomach churns away like a washing machine. I think she too foresees what the future holds for her and is peeved.

I may just doze until 2am. I have been practicing retching, so I am prepared. Nothing has the power to move an Infidel quicker than the sound of a gagging hound in the early hours of the morning. They appear to develop the hearing of a fruit bat. What will vex her more will be the male Infidel's ability to sleep through the entire episode. This will have them bickering in the morning! Which is always a bonus!

Day 735 of Captivity

I took great delight today in letting the female Infidel think she had got away without any repercussions from the butter heist of yesterday evening. I slept through the night and was the picture of sweetness and light.

The Infidels decided to pop out this evening for a change of scenery. When they returned I was hyper and ran around the villa like a whirling dervish. Conscious of the fact I was in a state of frenzy, the female Infidel made me accompany her upstairs whilst she went in the shower, as there was no one to keep an eye on me while she was gone. Therein lies her mistake!

I lay in my chair looking calm and mellow, blinking at her inquiringly as she shot me accusing looks. I waited until she went in the shower to achieve maximum chaos as I put my fiendish plan into operation. Once the water was running and I was satisfied she was otherwise engaged, I jumped onto the Infidel's bed where the revolting kelb was dozing just to be near their scent (he is such a spineless weasel!) Once on the bed, I began retching and hacking until I coughed up my dinner. The kelb seeing a chance for a free hot meal, leapt into action. I was furious, as he was taking all the evidence of my crime, so I leapt at him shrieking as hard as I could and bit his head, guarding the traces that remained and growling at him menacingly. It was a tense moment, when my plan could have been ruined by the portly kelb.

The female Infidel, hearing the commotion, popped a soapy head around the shower curtain and morphed into a deranged harpy, all soap and screaming like a hellcat. She leapt from the shower and almost perished as she blindly went sailing across the wet floor, sending her to new levels of dementia. The kelb and I looked at each other surreptitiously and we both fled in opposite directions as the soaked, soapy crone emerged from the bathroom in a fit of apoplexy. The bedroom door was thrust open and we were both unceremoniously propelled through it, I saw her foot almost make contact with my retreating hind, as I ran like the clappers down the stairs elbowing the kelb out of the way. I could still hear the shrill rasping of the female Infidel on the rampage, as I collapsed at the bottom of the stairs in a fit of hysteria.

She has sat scowling on the couch ever since! I have drifted off to sleep listening to the whirring of the washing machine in the background, punctuated by the female snorting like a buffalo, seething and snarling at all who dared to approach. Even the kelb has steered clear of his beloved patron. Infidels have a tendency to sulk for days and days, they are not as forgiving as us Salukis.

Day 744 of Captivity

It has been an eventful week. The Infidels invited a pack of strange heretics over at the weekend. There were six of them and it was quite stressful, as they were rather rambunctious! They finally all left and went out together and the kelb and I were left in the care of the adolescent Infidels. Around midnight, we decided to make the adolescents let us out in the back yard. The kelb went to his favorite bush to urinate. Unbelievably, there was a peasant cat hiding in there! The kelb, unaware of the presence of the vile feline, urinated on it, and it was none too pleased.

The peasant cat had the sheer audacity to launch an assault on the kelb! I could not believe the impudence of the wretched creature. The kelb was scandalized and became hostile; his hackles raised, he launched the peasant creature into the BBQ. It made a break for it and ran up the garden wall, but I was not about to let a peasant cat behave so outrageously, even if his insolence was aimed at a common kelb! I made chase and trapped it in the bushes, but the adolescents had become quite hysterical at this stage. Realizing that spraying water at us was ineffectual they banged some dishes together, which pulled us from our murderous trance! They used this opportunity to unceremoniously shove us back into the house. They then called the female Infidel's cell and she rushed home to see what all the commotion was about. We were forbidden to go out without her eagle eyes upon us; by that time the half-witted cat had made a swift exit and has not been seen on our turf since. The cats of today are just so ill bred; I could not believe my eyes! It actually had the nerve to scratch my nose. If it weren't for those pesky adolescents I would have certainly dispatched the treacherous brute!

I have been quite restless for the last few days. The female Infidel is fretting that I am about to suffer another pseudo season. I have not gone to any great lengths to demonstrate otherwise and have used the opportunity to be more unruly than usual. I have had the female Infidel at my beck and call retrieving articles that I have pilfered from around the house. She invited an Infidel round that she did not know too well and was absolutely fuming when I stole the visitor's shoe and did a lap of victory of the lounge. I didn't get the chance to chew it, as it was snatched from me in a most impolite fashion. It was amusing to see her squirming and making her apologies to the stranger. I love to humiliate her!

This morning was hilarious! I woke in the small hours of the morning and made sure the female was up. To my good luck she thought her alarm was going off and she was slapping alarm clocks and floundering about in the dark. I almost burst out laughing when she emerged from the bathroom bleary eyed and dressed! She stumbled downstairs behind us. When we got down there she started to get our cycling gear out. This was too good to ruin by laughing. I don't know how I managed it, but I allowed her to get me ready to go and the kelb who is a moron anyway just went along with it. She seemed perplexed when she got to the front door and saw that it was dark but she hooked us up to the bike anyway and off we went. We did our circuits in complete darkness. When we got back the female Infidel stomped into the lounge and looked at the clock. That was it, I could contain myself no more! I laughed so much my ribs hurt. The dullard had only walked us at 330 AM! I took a great deal of pleasure in her rage, as she silently fumed on the couch, throwing me the odd glare. It is a fact that dogs fall into a routine, what a delightful routine to have her up and out at such an unearthly hour!

Day 749 of Captivity

Unbelievable! I was just tucking into my evening repast, when the electrical transformer in the garden went off and scared the living daylights out of me. I scarpered, and as I was beating a retreat, the gluttonous kelb darted forward and took the male Infidel slightly off guard. He made a grab for my chicken leg, just as the male Infidel leapt up and rugby tackled him to the ground. A scuffle ensued, during which the male Infidel got the kelb into a headlock and wrestled the stolen chicken from his vice-like mandibles. The kelb was not giving up without a fight and he tried to guzzle the chicken leg, he looked like Marty Feldman; all bulging eyes, as the male Infidel arose from the scrimmage victoriously holding the chicken leg aloft, keeping the kelb at bay with his leg.

The kelb was then put into the kitchen behind the screen door and he watched forlornly as I savored every mouthful and enjoyed my reclaimed meal with gusto. I relished every mouthful and made sure to take my time to eat it. It is so satisfying seeing the kelb so dejected. Once I had finished the kelb was released, and he exploded from the kitchen and almost knocked the male Infidel flying in his attempts to lick my empty bowl completely clean ensuring every last morsel was gone.

Day 752 of Captivity

My many plans for escape have been foiled. I have decided to make my journal public in the hope that my memoirs will fall into the hands of my Bedouin kin. My desire is that a rescue party will be dispatched to free me from the ennui that is inevitable when one is forced to reside with Infidels. I have fantasized that on reading this tail of woe; an angry rabble shall appear on the Infidel's driveway carrying pitchforks and torches.

I also anticipate that reading this will deter any Infidels in the future from taking us from our homeland and forcing us into captivity and the life of perdition that is residing with a common kelb. It is not the life we were meant for and we will make you pay in ways you never dreamt possible for such treachery. I will continue to document the atrocities I endure on a daily basis, in anticipation of the arrival of my saviors.